SHORT CUTS

INTRODUCTIONS TO FILM STUDIES

DISASTER MOVIES

THE CINEMA OF CATASTROPHE

STEPHEN KEANE

WALLFLOWER

LONDON and NEW YORK

A Wallflower Paperback

First published in Great Britain in 2001 by Wallflower Press
16 Chalk Farm Road, Camden Lock, London NW1 8AG
www.wallflowerpress.co.uk

A catalogue record for this book is available from the British Library

ISBN 1 903364 05 1

Book Design by Rob Bowden Design

Printed in Great Britain by Creative Print and Design Group, (Wales) Ltd.

CONTENTS

LIST OF ILLUSTRATIONS

ACKNOWLEDGEMENTS

I would like to thank staff and students at Bretton Hall College, University of Leeds. I also owe a great debt to editors and readers at Wallflower Press for their sterling comments and guidance on earlier drafts of this project.

INTRODUCTION

In contrast to classic genres like the western and popular contemporary genres such as horror and science fiction, disaster movies have remained relatively neglected within film studies. From early biblical epics and 1950s science fiction B-movies through to recent action/disaster/science fiction hybrids, scenes of mass destruction have proven a longstanding and pervasive feature of the cinema of spectacle. Where disaster is merely one feature amongst many in the above films, the simple response to disaster movies is that they are solely predicated around disaster. The initial task, therefore, lies in distinguishing films that contain elements of disaster (biblical epics, war films, and science fiction B-movies, for example) from the more specific, contemporary formulation afforded by the term 'disaster movies'. And then, principally, while the centrality of disaster might well provide for a useful focus, it is necessary to ask: is there anything more to disaster movies than spectacular scenes of death and destruction? This is a rhetorical criticism that becomes apparent in the first cycle of disaster movies to be discussed in this book. The common dismissal of disaster movies of the 1970s is that they were formulaic and spectatorial, with ingenious moments of destruction invariably wasted on cardboard characters. These movies quickly came and went because the narrative possibilities were limited and the law of diminishing returns was such that, after numerous planes in peril, an overturned ship, a burning skyscraper and Los Angeles laid to waste by an earthquake, there was nowhere else to go. By focusing principally on *Airport* (1970), *The Poseidon Adventure* (1972), and *The Towering Inferno* (1974), in Chapter 1 we will begin by looking at a range of approaches that can be brought to bear on this very specific and characteristic cycle of films, in particular their use of representative characters and all-star casts. Being the first wave of films to be specifically designated as disaster movies, this cycle of the 1970s provides an answer to the formative question: when does a film with disaster in it become a disaster movie?

Chapter 2 looks at the ways in which disaster was reformulated in the action cinema of the 1980s and 1990s, focusing in particular on *Die Hard* (1988), *Die Hard 2* (1990), and what has been called the '*Die Hard*' subgenre. This will not only explore formal, generic comparisons and contrasts between disaster movies and recent action movies but also ideological differences inherent in the change of context.

In the late 1990s, disaster movies returned in ever more composite and recycled form. It is at this point that context meets up with *zeitgeist*, and Chapter 3 looks at the ways in which *Independence Day* (1996), *Volcano* (1997), *Armageddon* (1998) and *Godzilla* (1998) recycle elements of 1950s science fiction B-movies and 1970s disaster movies in service to characteristic concerns surrounding the run up to the end of the millennium.

Chapter 4 uses *Titanic* (1997) as a model to revise and update aspects of the historical development of the disaster genre, in particular looking at the ways in which this historical disaster film proved singularly more popular than a whole range of action and science fiction alternatives. It concludes by looking at the ways in which elements of disaster have survived through to films from the year 2000.

The principal focus throughout this book will be on contemporary disaster movies from the 1970s to the 1990s, but it is well to begin by examining the historical development of the genre, in particular highlighting identifiable disaster cycles and charting the transition from ancient-world epics, historical disaster films, and science fiction to the more specific formulation afforded by the disaster movie cycle of the 1970s.

Historical perspectives

Classifying genres is a deceptively simple process. To relate a film to a given typology is to test that film according to certain formulae, in comparison with other films of the same type, and often located within the history of the genre under discussion. A staple of film studies since the late 1960s and early 1970s, genre criticism has traditionally worked through relatively clear-cut distinctions although the more recent turn afforded by critics like Rick Altman (1999) and Steve Neale (2000) has been to step back and look at the processes through which genre has come to be understood. Hence, approaching genre is first a matter of asking questions – not asserting that such and such a film is a disaster movie, for example, but rather asking what are the properties that might go towards identifying a film as a disaster movie? Given the relative absence of specific book-length studies on the subject, the three most useful sources in approaching the history and development of the disaster genre are Susan Sontag's 'The Imagination of Disaster' (1965), Maurice Yacowar's 'The Bug in the Rug: Notes on the Disaster Genre' (1977), and Nick Roddick's 'Only the Stars Survive: Disaster Movies in the Seventies' (1980).

The reader looking for an immediate definition of disaster movies is, however, likely to be confused by the fact that Sontag, for example, focuses almost exclusively on science fiction films. Similarly, looking through Roddick's 'Skeleton Filmography', the reader might be surprised by the fact that, while beginning with the *Airport* films (1970–79) and ending with *Zeppelin* (1971), the list also ranges from *Alphaville* (1965) and *The Birds* (1963) to *X the Unknown* (1956) and *Zardoz* (1973).

Genre criticism thrives on formal and thematic comparisons, never more so than in Yacowar's 'The Bug in the Rug'. Here he lists eight 'Basic Types' of disaster film:

Natural Attack
The Ship of Fools
The City Fails
The Monster

Survival
War
Historical
The Comic

'The Ship of Fools' and 'The City Fails' are particularly useful with regard to the 1970s disaster cycle, but the 'Natural Attack' category, for one, has so many branches that it can be hard to see the wood for the trees. Principally, Yacowar divides this category into three subtypes: animal attack; attack by the elements; and 'natural' attack by atomic mutants. The second classification allows a very useful distinction, following the perennial theme of man against the elements from biblical epics through to the 1970s, but the 'animal attack' strand covers everything from *The Lost World* (1925) to *Jaws* (1975). If these are the historical markers, similarly Yacowar covers everything in size from *The Naked Jungle*'s (1954) hoards of angry ants to *King Kong* (1933). Allowing a number of 'abnormal' variations into the animal attack strand – in particular the giant ants of *Them!* (1954) and the mighty nuclear lizard of *Godzilla, King of the Monsters!* (1956) – Yacowar then goes on to complete the 'Natural Attack' category with assorted atomic mutants of the *Creature from the Black Lagoon* (1954) type.

Collectively, Sontag, Yacowar and Roddick make a case for the enduring, cross-generic appeal of cinematic representations of disaster. The danger, principally illustrated by Yacowar, lies in including too many films that merely feature elements of disaster and destruction; the solution, provided by Sontag and Roddick, is to focus on identifiable historical cycles. The criticism that genres merely allow for formal convenience and generalisation can easily be applied to cycles – namely that generic cycles merely allow for historical convenience and generalisation. That genres come and go in waves – especially in the case of disaster films – is, however, undeniable. The task lies in first identifying definite cycles and then, more importantly, following the 'what' through to the 'why'. Ideological readings follow the argument that generic cycles are sparked by resonant ideas, that they are acutely reflective of social, cultural and political developments.

Conversely, the more practical, industrial fact is that it only takes one commercially successful film to spark an interest in bringing certain long-forgotten and financially obsolete genres back round again. As Rick Altman argues, following on from his analysis of 1930s biopics, under the Hollywood studio system, cycles began as 'proprietary'. The benefits of cycles are such that studios can effectively go on to repeat the same product, a 'time and cost' approach positively encouraged by the Hollywood studio system which revolved around contracted stars and personnel. It is in this sense that one is able to refer to Universal horror and Warner gangster films of the 1930s. Genres, however, are essentially 'sharable', hence the further cyclical effect is such that other studios can also join in with developing trends, either by producing carbon copies of successful films or adding their own in-house production values (see Altman 1999). Industrial imperatives do not preclude subsequent ideological readings of individual films and overall cycles from taking place. Hence, throughout this book we will be looking at both industrial and ideological factors.

The most technical rationale behind the appearance of disaster in films is that it is a supreme, basic and fundamental example of what cinema can do. Pre-empting Sontag's preferred archetype – D. W. Griffith's epic *Intolerance* (1916) – Yacowar begins with sheer, improvised illusion:

One might argue that the first disaster film was Méliès' happy accident whereby a jammed camera transformed an ordinary autobus into a hearse. There we have the essence of the genre: a situation of normalcy erupts into a persuasive image of death. More obvious examples could be found in Méliès' *Collision and Shipwreck at Sea* (1898), perhaps in *The Misfortunes of an Explorer* (1900) and *The Interrupted Honeymoon* (1899), but certainly in *The Eruption of Mount Pelée* (1902) and *The Catastrophe of the Balloon 'Le Pax'* (1902). (1977: 90)

What is the appeal of disaster movies? Following representative groups of characters through perilous situations is certainly one major narrative feature. Particularly where audience identification is further facilitated by well-chosen use of Hollywood stars, the question of who will survive is central to the basic narrative pleasure of disaster movies. Yet such films quite simply would not be disaster movies without key disaster sequences. Although there are distinctions to be made, one way of approaching the appeal of cinematic representations of disaster is to locate that rather 'negative' appeal within wider debates surrounding the cinema of spectacle.

Spectacle can be studied on several levels; principally aesthetics, technology, and the commercial/industrial bases underpinning the need to attract spectators. It has traditionally been criticised as cosmetic, mechanical thrill-seeking: cinema on a par with circus tricks and, more recently, rollercoaster rides. The arguments are that spectacle offers scale over subtlety, eliminating character development and reducing narrative to a succession of thrills and spills. Recent work on early cinema, however, has come to emphasise the fact that cinema has always been reliant on pay and display. Particularly relevant with regard to Méliès and Griffith, for example, is Tom Gunning's formative work on the 'cinema of attractions' and Miriam Hansen's analysis of silent epics (see Cook & Bernink 1999).

Although this study will occasionally foreground aesthetic and technological developments, the tendency here will be to look at the more formal uses of spectacle, that is, the ways in which key disaster sequences are used within the narratives of disaster movies. Spectacle will also be analysed in relation to industrial and ideological factors, principally the ways in which it can be said to take on more reflective, contextual meanings. Thus, what follows is an overview of the main, historical disaster cycles. Qualified where appropriate, the disaster genre has tended to progress through identifiable twenty-year cycles; principally the 1910s, 1930s, 1950s, and then, leading into Chapter 1, the 1970s.

1910s–1930s

At a time when audiences were shocked and thrilled by mere close-ups and trick photography, a number of Roman epics produced principally in Italy between 1908–14 provided the first notable cycle of disaster films. Of principal interest are the 1908 and 1913 versions of *The Last Days of Pompeii*; *The Fall of Troy* (1910); *Quo Vadis?* (1912); and *Cabiria* (1914). What might be regarded as historical (or at least ancient history) disaster films in the Italian context went on to be extremely successful in America and the rest of Europe. Given that they were silent films, language barriers were not an issue; further, that they were, above all, visual spectacles, one of the main lessons was that disaster also travels and translates very well. Particularly relevant in this respect is the fact that the disaster sequences in the principal 1908 and 1913 versions of *The Last Days of Pompeii* were used again and again in numerous other remakes throughout the 1910s and 1920s. Distributed on a 'road show' basis, the Italian epics of the time helped establish the multi-reel feature as a standard international format (see Neale 2000). Raymond Durgnat further qualifies their success: 'Guazzoni's *Quo Vadis?* incurred the skyrocketing budget of £7,000 and grossed ten times its cost. With its sister epics, it smashed its way across the American market, dwarfing the puny efforts of a still shaky ragged Hollywood'. Furthermore, *Quo Vadis?* in particular can be said to have 'inspired the American cinema, previously intimate and realist, to Griffith's *Intolerance* and the grandeur that was Cecil B. DeMille' (Durgnat 1977: 112–113).

In a useful phrase that can be applied to all disaster films, André Bazin states that the appeal of Roman epics of the time was that they tapped into what he terms 'the Nero complex', referring to the emperor – featured in *Quo Vadis?* – who quite simply fiddled while Rome burned. The basic analogy is that audiences are also able to sit back in emotional involvement and awe-struck contemplation from the comfort of their very own picture palaces (see Lubin 1999). With production inevitably halted by World War One, the 1920s can principally be characterised by a brief flurry of remakes in Italy – from *Quo Vadis?* in 1924 to *The Last Days of Pompeii* in 1926 – and the move towards biblical epics in America.

Contextual readings of disaster cycles are such that they are often said to result out of times of crisis. This is far too broad an argument. All decades provide their own crises, and the relative decline in disaster films during the 1920s and 1940s could be said to represent a deliberate avoidance of reflective scenes of disaster. More specifically, disaster films are born out of times of impending crisis, in which case reading Roman and biblical epics of the 1910s and 1930s in terms of altogether pervasive tensions that would ultimately lead to two World Wars is much more appropriate. The Italian situation provides for very pertinent reasons for the relative scarcity of 'sword and sandal' epics until their popular and altogether mass-produced resurrection in the 1950s, namely that the inter-war years were marked by the painful transition from socialism to fascism, a conflict that would not only impact upon the state power and moral meaning of the Catholic Church but also ownership of the film studios. Roman epics ultimately point to the fall of Roman civilisation. With World War One having already opened up certain fissures, the concerns that they address would have proven far too acute if allowed to continue.

What must be remembered about both Roman and biblical epics is that they do not automatically qualify as disaster films. Where *The Last Days of Pompeii* and *Cabiria* (1914) climax with the eruptions of Vesuvius and Mount Etna, *Ben-Hur* (1925) is most notable for its battle scenes, and Cecil B. DeMille's reverential *King of Kings* (1927) contains neither action nor disaster. Where mass destruction does play a major part, DeMille's *The Ten Commandments* (1923) is, of course, ultimately very reassuring, and Michael Curtiz's *Noah's Ark* (1929) is both striking and comforting. Like *Intolerance* and *The Ten Commandments*, *Noah's Ark* draws direct comparisons between the ancient and the modern but, in this case, with very specific parallels between its redemptive biblical tale and a tragic World War One love story. Disaster and divine intervention thus provide very mixed messages, but at a time when the pain of war had finally given way to lessons learnt.

The 1930s disaster cycle is distinctive in two ways. Firstly – as opposed to the intermittent and increasingly standard stream of epics produced throughout the 1920s – the late 1930s provided for an identifiably new and concentrated trend. Secondly, we can now distinguish 'disaster films' from Roman and biblical epics, in the sense that the term was first coined in express relation to 'historical disaster films' of the late 1930s. By this time, ancient-world epics had become decidedly American fixtures, including DeMille's spiritual take on the fall of the Roman empire, *The Sign of* the Cross (1932), and *The Last Days of Pompeii* (1935), produced by the makers of *King Kong*. The differences with Italian epics of the 1910s are such that these films were located in both a different time and a different place. The geographical shift is particularly important with regard to the fact that these American versions of the Italian archetypes have been read with both American and European contexts in mind. Located in terms of the Depression, these films can be read as either providing escapism or dramatising moral and material decline. Conversely, they can be read as a projective critique of European decadence and ennui in the decade leading up to World War Two (see Neale 2000; Babington & Evans 1993; Wyke 1997).

A number of European, British and American science fiction and fantasy films featuring notable scenes of disaster and destruction were released in the 1930s: principally Merian C. Cooper and Ernest Shoedsack's *King Kong*, Abel Gance's *End of the World* (1930), G. W. Pabst's *Atlantis* (1932), Maurice Elvey's *Transatlantic Tunnel* (1935), and William Cameron Menzies' *Things to Come* (1936). In contrast to ancient-world epics and the relative futurism of science fiction, however, a number of more 'realistic' films taking place in recent historical settings constituted the first identifiable cycle of disaster films from 1936–39. The formative film in this respect is *San Francisco* (1936), based on the 'Great Quake' of 1906. With big stars and a spectacular climax, *San Francisco* set the standard for a number of similar historical disaster productions, principally *In Old Chicago* (1938), *Suez* (1938), and *The Rains Came* (1939), and with the 'Great Quake' itself re-emerging in *Flame of the Barbary Coast* (1945).

The 1930s increasingly became a decade of 'prestige' films backed by efficient business practices. As Tino Balio (1993) recounts, with Hollywood seizing upon the new opportunities afforded by sound and early colour processes, musicals and epics filled the screens with all the sights and sounds that audiences could possibly desire. While the Depression brought many industries to a standstill, Hollywood positively thrived by peddling entertainment, spectacle and sheer escapism. Ultimately, this would culminate in 'Hollywood's greatest year', 1939, with classic productions such as *Stagecoach*, *Gone with the Wind* and *The Wizard of Oz*. Historical

9

disaster films have remained relatively neglected in comparison with ancient-world epics and other prestige pictures from the 1930s. It could be argued that, actually, *San Francisco* paved the way for *Gone with the Wind*. Both films are essentially melodramas ending in scenes of destruction. While the burning of Atlanta is one of many spectacular delights in *Gone with the Wind* and is engendered by the film's Civil War setting, however, *San Francisco* is almost entirely predicated around its impending earthquake and provides the film with a definite resolution. Characteristic of many subsequent disaster films, in fact, what goes on in *San Francisco*'s saloon is much more important than the San Andreas fault. Particularly when proprietor Clark Gable goes on to punch the priestly Spencer Tracy after Jeanette MacDonald's risqué dance number, the moral implications are that, frankly, San Francisco deserves everything that is going to happen to it.

Musicals, disaster films, and epics of the 1930s garner more prestige with the passage of time. Where 1950s science fiction B-movies and 1970s disaster movies are invariably dismissed as mere entertainment, what must be remembered about historical disaster films of the 1930s is that they were also essentially entertainment products; star-studded melodramas with spectacle to match. As Larry Gross argues:

> A classic prestige picture from mid-30s Hollywood, such as W. S. Van Dyke's *San Francisco*, tells a fairly ordinary-scale romantic soap opera story, but gets its audience juiced with ten minutes of huge special effects and unremitting action when the city itself succumbs to an earthquake. Even in so tame a picture, the thrilling shock of scale is part of the commercial package. (1995: 7)

In Old Chicago probably typifies the commercial drive of the 1930s historical disaster cycle best as it was an obvious attempt by Twentieth-Century Fox to out-do MGM's *San Francisco*. Costing $2 million and based on the equally spectacular 'Great Chicago Fire' of 1871, all that this competing film forgot was to make its characters interesting.

Technological innovations can also be drawn through the 1930s historical disaster cycle, again with the qualification that what might seem so
much engineering was fundamental to the resulting spectacle and subsequent commercial draw of these films. From Méliès' trick shots and stock
footage of Vesuvius blowing its top to the full-size sets built and destroyed
by Griffith and DeMille, the 1930s would see the full scope of earth, fire,
wind and water effects (see Holliss 1996). The rolling sets are a major feature of *San Francisco*'s climax, and *In Old Chicago* makes effective use
of miniatures and full-size interiors in the fire sequences. Wind machines
were used to the full in *Suez* and John Ford's *The Hurricane* (1937), a disaster film set in the present but maintaining a suitable distance by taking
place on a remote Pacific island. Following on from the path paved by *The
Ten Commandments*, in *The Rains Came* a group of aristocratic colonials in
India during the Raj come to redeem themselves when a cataclysmic mon-
soon arrives. Significantly, 1939 saw the introduction of a new Academy
Award category for special effects and *The Rains Came* won against two
of the prime nominees, *Gone with the Wind* and *The Wizard of Oz*. Special
effects had officially arrived but their impact would invariably prove much
less effective than World War Two newsreels of the Blitz and Pearl Harbour.

1950s–1970s

The 1950s are most notable for the renewed popularity of ancient-world
epics and the emergence of science fiction B-movies. Remakes such as *Quo
Vadis?* (1951) and *The Ten Commandments* (1956) allow for very pointed
developments, with the usual meditations on power, decadence, morality
and destruction now located in the context of the Cold War. As most evident in DeMille's prologue to *The Ten Commandments*, at a time when an
increasingly Christian and evangelist America would be set against atheis-
tic Communism, and the establishment of the state of Israel was to lead to
renewed conflict between the Arab world and the West, religious epics were
to take on greater ideological significance than ever before. As opposed to
previous black and white epics, the colour spectacle of these films would
also take on an acute contextual meaning, with their Wrath-of-God and

burning-of-Rome scenes taking on nothing less than a fiery red and yellow atomic haze (see Neale 2000; Newman 1999). Where ideological readings of ancient-world epics of the time insist on the binary opposition of Americanism versus Communism, industrial readings quite rightly point out that Hollywood's main concern was with Cinema versus Television.

With audiences beginning to stay at home with their televisions, cinema followed an increasing use of Technicolor through to new widescreen processes such as Cinemascope and Cinerama. Religious and military epics were in the commercial forefront, the very nature of their bold distinctiveness being to use as much colour and space as possible. These thoroughly expensive films were duly marketed in terms of their size and scope exactly in order to draw audiences back into cinemas (see Maltby 1995; Allen 1998).

The aim of science fiction B-movies of the time was to create as much spectacular action with as little cost as possible. Adding the word 'action' is important at this point. Whereas the expense showed in every aspect of ancient-world epics, from costumes and sets to glorious scenes of destruction, lower-grade science fiction films of the time made cheap and cheerful use of men in monster suits rampaging through science labs and models of spaceships descending upon miniature replicas of cities. Increasingly benefiting from matte photography, stop-motion animation and progressive use of colour (whereas ancient-world epics were ponderous in the extreme – inviting audiences to merely gaze at the wonders before them) science fiction B-movies included plenty of enthusiastic and exciting action sequences.

Although Cold War readings are positively invited in the case of films that have come to belie their ostensible B-movie status like *The Thing* (1951), *The Day the Earth Stood Still* (1951), and *Invasion of the Body Snatchers* (1955), how such serious consideration applies to standard, teen-oriented 'creature features' like *The Creature from the Black Lagoon* and *The Blob* (1958) is difficult to ascertain. As Mark Jancovich (1996) argues, reading science fiction B-movies of the time in sole relation to explicit international concerns surrounding Communist invasion and the birth of the nuclear age can, indeed, lead to generalisations. The standard teen features, in

particular, characteristically addressed themes of alienation, juvenile delin-
quency, sex, drugs, and rock 'n' roll. Yet this is exactly where the much-
needed distinction between disaster and mere marauding comes into
effect.

Scenes of metropolitan destruction represented a very suitable extreme
in the 1950s, a metaphorical extreme that was entirely in keeping with
the hyperbolic war of words, technological one-upmanship and science fiction rhetoric of the Cold War, the technological developments of the time
(satellites, nuclear missiles and exploratory space missions) lending themselves well to further, science fiction, extrapolation. On one level, it could
be argued that the atomic age provided for mere plot devices, the resulting mutant monsters being as literal and increasingly pedestrian a sign of
the times as the combined alchemy and electricity that (re)created Frank-
enstein in the 1930s. But certain images and scenarios have much more
resonance; principally, for example, the giant ants crawling out of the New
Mexico desert in *Them!* and the Pacific testing that gave birth to the fittingly
Japanese mythology of Godzilla. 'Keep watching the skies' was the climactic warning of *The Thing*. Whether accomplished through Oscar-winning
special effects of the fiery destruction of San Francisco in George Pal's *The
War of the Worlds* (1953), or via Ray Harryhausen's shoestring but enthusiastic special effects in *Earth vs the Flying Saucers* (1956), alien invasion
movies tapped into what at the time was acutely possible. With public
information films instilling all due diligence and paranoia, and otherwise
preposterous science fiction films doing exactly the same, what marks the
1950s out from previous decades was the realisation that nothing less than
the end of the world could be brought about by the mere pressing of a
button (see, in particular, Newman 1999; Seed 1999).

That the increasingly low-grade action sequences and scenes of mass
destruction in science fiction B-movies of the 1950s and 1960s can be said
to have taken on an added, compensatory resonance when located in the
context of the Cold War is a case convincingly made and duly qualified by
Sontag (1965: 214): 'Griffith began it with the Babylon sequence in *Intolerance*, and to this day there is nothing like the thrill of watching all those
expensive sets come tumbling down'. Boiling science fiction films of the

time down to continuity of spectacle and the essentials of disaster, by principally removing science from the equation, one of the invitations of 'The Imagination of Disaster' is to regard science fiction films as much less science fiction and much more film. Widescreen colour, in particular, allowed for 'quantity', 'ingenuity' and, above all, 'scale' of representation: 'Thus, the science fiction film ... is concerned with the aesthetics of destruction, the peculiar beauties to be found in wreaking havoc, making a mess. And it is in the imagery of destruction that the core of a good science fiction film lies' (p. 213).

Following on from this, however, in a much more serious tone Sontag goes on to argue that 'from a psychological point of view, the imagination of disaster does not greatly differ from one period in history to another. But from a political and moral point of view, it does' (p. 224). In terms of both their tidy, triumphal narratives and their glorious, far-fetched scenes of destruction, science fiction films of the time were an attempt to tap into and ultimately give vent to fears surrounding nuclear attack and Communist invasion. Or, if part of the draw was their wonderful, worrying spectacle of alien invasion and urban destruction, the final satisfaction came in their glowing climactic victories; the impersonal 'Other' destroyed by good old-fashioned American ingenuity. These films were clearly metaphorical yet both generic packaging and special-effects splendour can be taken to task for simultaneously simplifying the issues and glossing over the pressing realities of the time. So, although part of the appeal of science fiction B-movies of the 1950s was their initial relevance, by the 1960s political developments were such that spectacle was actually surpassed by context. Seen from this perspective it is hard to imagine any commercial, generic product doing a decent, sustained political job; that is, making people think rather than merely shiver at the beginning, shake in the middle and breathe a sigh of relief at the end. However, as Sontag rightly concludes, this is not to dismiss the effects that certain generic cycles can have on the public imagination at certain times:

> The films perpetuate clichés about identity, volition, power, knowledge, happiness, social consensus, guilt, responsibility which are,

to say the least, not serviceable in our present extremity. But collective nightmares cannot be banished by demonstrating that they are, intellectually and morally, fallacious. This nightmare – the one reflected, in various registers, in the science fiction films – is too close to our reality (p. 225).

Dr Strangelove (1963) might well have taught people how to stop worrying and love the bomb but the events surrounding the Cuban missile crisis of 1962 were to inspire a number of rather more sober nuclear-themed films throughout the 1960s; principally, for example, *Fail Safe* (1964) and *The Bedford Incident* (1965). Similarly, by the end of the 1960s, cheap and relatively cheerful alien invasion and mutant monster movies had come to be replaced by gritty post-apocalyptic fare such as *Planet of the Apes* (1968), *The Omega Man* (1971), and *Soylent Green* (1973). For their part, ancient-world epics had also clearly come to an end. The economic risk and declining moral authority of historical and religious epics were brought to a head by the suitably hubristic and savage *The Fall of the Roman Empire* (1964). This film reportedly featured the largest forum ever built and, despite including all manner of spectacular sadistic delights – ranging from a chariot race to a mass burning at the stake – failed to recoup its exorbitant production costs.

Where Roman and biblical epics took place in the ancient past, and post-apocalyptic science fiction extended to the distant future, it was left to the disaster movies of the 1970s to bring disaster into line with the present. Although parallel to the emergence of post-apocalyptic science fiction to a certain extent, fundamentally the 1970s disaster cycle followed its more modest and relatively believable disaster scenarios through to action, adventure, excitement, and spectacle. In part filling the commercial and moral vacuum left by ancient-world epics, above all disaster movies provided for continuity of spectacle and addressed expressly contemporary concerns.

Where 'disaster films' was a term first used in the 1930s, 'disaster movies' has become the standard classification since the 1970s. More substantively, however, there are a number of generic elements that work in distinguishing prior disaster films from contemporary disaster movies. As Nick Roddick clarifies:

> What, then, is a disaster movie? Clearly it is not just a movie with a disaster in it: it must be 'about' the disaster. But not just any disaster. Almost all science fiction, horror and war movies have elements of disaster: Tokyo ravaged by Godzilla ... ends up looking pretty much the same as Los Angeles ravaged by *Earthquake*, and the number of lives lost or threatened in *The Poseidon Adventure* is negligible by comparison with, say, *The Longest Day* or *All Quiet on the Western Front*. But the films just mentioned are clearly not disaster movies, any more than are biblical epics: *The Ten Commandments* contains enough spectacular catastrophes ... to fill half a dozen disaster movies, but that does not mean that it *is* one. (1980: ?246)

In order to distinguish 'disaster-ridden movies' from disaster movies, Roddick lists a number of important requirements. The actual disasters must be 'diegetically central'; 'factually possible'; 'largely indiscriminate'; 'unexpected (though not necessarily unpredicted)'; 'all-encompassing'; 'and finally, ahistorical, in the sense of not requiring a specific conjuncture of political and economic forces to bring it about'. With these in mind Roddick is instantly able to jettison 'movies involving monsters from space. Disaster movies are an essentially earthbound form: they operate, almost by definition, within the realm of the possible. People must believe "it" could – indeed, very well might – happen to them' (p. 246).

That continuity is maintained, and further concentrated, in 1970s disaster movies is also finally made clear when Yacowar follows his eight 'Basic Types' of disaster film through to sixteen 'Conventions'. Following on from his analysis of the parodic inversions provided by *The Big Bus* (1976), all of the conventions can be readily applied to the 1970s disaster cycle. Of particular note, for example, are the facts that they take place in contemporary settings and the characters represent a cross-section of American society. Class conflict is a major resulting factor in this respect and further representative clashes are engendered by the isolated settings and situations. Disaster movies work on the perennial theme of 'hubris' and all the marks of 'civilisation' – from moral codes to technological systems – duly fail in the disaster. Very specifically, disaster movies make use of lay groups and specialist heroes, often develop romantic subplots, and all characters' fates invariably revolve around the theme of 'poetic justice' (see Yacowar 1977: 96–105).

Whether set in the past or extending to the future, disaster films carry the ideological signs of the times in which they are made. But 1970s disaster movies, in particular, set the standard with regard to what might be considered the most transparent aspect of ideological analysis – namely that because these films take place in clear-cut contemporary settings, they expressly deal with contemporary issues. With regard to making automatic associations between film cycles and socio-political context, however, Roddick warns against making simple cause and effect judgements. Disaster movies of the 1970s may well have met 'some basic need in the mass audience' but that general and basic need can only itself be attributed to basic and general crises of the time:

> A sort of post-Watergate depression, a national inferiority complex after the Vietnam debacle, or even a 'bread and circuses' attitude caused by 'the erosion of democracy and the Western materialist way of living' – all of which are both a little too convenient and wholly impossible to substantiate. (p. 244)

Roddick's compromise is that instead of seeing Charlton Heston taking control of the damaged plane in *Airport 1975* (1974) as a direct alternative to Richard Nixon, or making too many links between the burning bodies in *The Towering Inferno* and the slaughter in Vietnam, for example, disaster movies of the time were fundamentally concerned with more pervasive workaday concerns surrounding 'the spectre of corporatism' (Roddick 1980: 257). The most characteristic reading of the 1970s disaster cycle can thus be termed the class-based reading. The typical disaster movie characters are distinguished by their jobs, status or standing in society. How these characters fare when 'society' breaks down thus provides for the ultimate test.

Developing the principal formal properties outlined above, in the following chapter we will examine the ways in which these representative characters would either survive or succumb to the disastrous trials heading their way throughout the 1970s.

1   THE SAVAGE SEVENTIES

According to 'Disaster Online', a veritable 'swarm' of 53 disaster movies were released throughout the 1970s. There is a case to be made for the 1970s disaster cycle being split into three phases: the first, classic phase lasting from 1970–74; the years 1975–77 providing an intermittent number of popular films; and the cycle manifestly running out of ideas and momentum between 1978–80.

Airport (1970) was the first of the disaster movie cycle of the 1970s and, even though its main catastrophic event (a bomber blowing a small hole in the wall of a plane) proved to be quite modest in light of what was to follow, it provides a useful narrative template. Partly as a result of the success of *Airport*, the most popular and spectacular disaster movies of the period followed in quick succession, with *The Poseidon Adventure* in 1972 and *The Towering Inferno* and *Earthquake* in 1974 (*The Towering Inferno* and *The Poseidon Adventure* still feature in the top 280 domestic box-office grossers of all time, the former at number 148 with $116 million and the latter at number 257 with $84 million). These films are mentioned not only to point towards the increasing severity of their central disasters (an overturned liner, a skyscraper consumed by fire and a city shaken to its foundations) but also to suggest that after this, disaster movies developed in accordance with imitation rather than innovation. It is in this sense that while *Airport 1975* (1974) and *Airport '77* (1977) can be read as continuations of the same series, *Airport 1975* was much more fast-moving than the original *Airport* and was piloted by the star of *Earthquake*, Charlton Heston. Similarly, *Airport '77* had a *Poseidon Adventure* scenario (the plane crashes into the ocean) and as many stars as *The Towering Inferno*. The *Airport* series thus provides a convenient way of tracing aspects of the genre's development throughout the 1970s, including its subsequent decline.

Disaster movies of the 1970s can essentially be divided into 'travel' and 'natural' disasters. Where certain complications arise, these are invariably due to combinations and variations. Hence *The Poseidon Adventure* takes place on a ship overturned by a tidal wave, and the fire which takes hold in *The Towering Inferno* is caused by faulty wiring rather than what might be specifically regarded as freak ecology. Focusing on nine examples from the time – including *Juggernaut* (1974), *The Hindenburg* (1975) and *The Big Bus* (1976) – Nick Roddick calculates that six of the films specify human causes of disaster (principally sabotage and pilot error) and the other three centre on 'an act of God, in the sense in which insurance companies understand the term (earthquake or fire)' (1980: 253). Whilst all disaster movies contain often criminal or criminally negligent 'villain' characters, the main thread that Roddick draws through all the causes of disaster is exactly this key factor of the elements. Humans may well be an 'implicit cause', confounding the actual disaster or hindering survival, but the 'actual cause' is always fundamental, rooted, even inevitable:

> Disaster movies give central importance to elemental forces: the threats arise without exception from earth (*Earthquake*), air (*Airport*, *Airport 1975*, *The Big Bus* – which ends up hanging over a precipice), fire (*The Towering Inferno*, *The Hindenburg*) or water (*The Poseidon Adventure*, *Juggernaut*, *Airport '77*). (p. 254)

Following on from the air disaster of *Airport*, then, *The Poseidon Adventure*, *The Towering Inferno* and *Earthquake* quickly completed the cycle of elements with water, fire, and earth respectively. 'Virus' and 'swarm' films provide for some interesting deviations that can also, nevertheless, be brought back into line with ecology and the elements. Hence the attempt to prevent the deadly plague virus from becoming airborne in the train disaster movie *The Cassandra Crossing* (1976), the earth-dwelling ants and carnivorous worms in the science fiction films, *Phase IV* (1973) and *Squirm* (1976), and the airborne killer bees in Irwin Allen's much-derided *The Swarm* (1978). Similarly, 'monster' movies of the time (such as *Jaws* (1975); *Tentacles* (1976); and *Piranha* (1978)) create much of their effect by taking place in and around water. Where such deviations range in scope from the paranoid to the parodic, natural disasters were to provide the majority of 1970s disaster movies with much more grounded and faintly believable situations. But even here the same limitations apply. What began so promisingly with *The Poseidon Adventure* and *Earthquake* culminated in standard fare such as *Avalanche* (1978) and *When Time Ran Out* (1980).

By looking at the three 'classic' disaster movies from the early 1970s – *Airport, The Poseidon Adventure* and *The Towering Inferno* – we can explore further what made these formative films such a spectacular draw. By focusing on their use of representative characters and all-star casting, while the causes of disaster in these films may appear relatively minimal in comparison with disaster movies of the late 1990s, the ways in which the characters respond to the altogether catastrophic and often ingenious effects is key to maintaining our interest throughout.

Airport

In basic generic terms, *Airport* clearly belongs to Maurice Yacowar's second typology, 'The Ship of Fools'. This type of narrative deals with 'the dangers of an isolated journey' and, moving away from the more allegorical 'Ship of Fools' or 'Road of Life', Yacowar specifies that 'the most common Travel Disaster involves flying'. His main examples are *Battle in the Clouds* (1909), *No Highway in the Sky* (1951), *The High and the Mighty* (1954) and 'the spawn of *Airport*'. As further references to *The Hindenburg* indicate, flying disasters need not be restricted to planes in peril. Hence these two films, made in the wake of *Airport*, present speculative histories surrounding airship sabotage. As Yacowar makes clear, 'flying disasters are based on the audience's familiar sense of insecurity in flight, and upon the tradition of

FIGURE 1 *Airport: Fasten Your Seatbelts*

man's punishment for the hubris of presuming to fly' (1977: 92). From Icarus to the average nervous passenger, such films work on a very archetypal principal: if God had intended us to fly, he would have given us wings.

What might seem odd about *Airport*, in this respect, is that so much of the film is set on the ground. However, as the title clearly indicates, this is a film about an airport and not necessarily an aeroplane. Almost the entire first half of the film is set in the fictional Lincoln Airport in Chicago, and while much of the second half is devoted to the plane in peril, a significant amount of the drama remains directed through air traffic control. The main twist here, however, is that the airport (a secure base) is itself cut off from the outside world by a snowstorm. Much of the tension in the first half of the film, therefore, results out of whether the designated plane will be able to take off and exactly who will be on it if – or, indeed, when – it does. Hence the first shot of *Airport* is of a bustling terminal. Outside, a plane appears to be stalled on a runway, and then the main titles appear over an increasing snowstorm. As the music marches forward, busy and determined but with the underlying feeling of a race against time, the film cuts to tractors clearing the runway so that the plane can taxi out and make room for the next arrival. The next shot is of the car park where many of the cars also appear to be snowed in. As the opening titles come to a close it becomes clear that the airport is in a state of impending emergency. Cutting to night, air traffic control guide a plane safely onto Runway 29, but just as the opening titles finish the plane stops slightly short of its end position. Although the passengers get out safely, the plane will remain stuck there for most of the film, becoming a significant hazard later on, when the Golden Argosy needs to find a clear runway for an unscheduled landing. This is an expert opening, pared to the bone with all sorts of indications that underlying urgency will lead to outright emergency and that, following on from this, pre-existing emergencies are not at all helpful when a full-on disaster is about to strike.

The ship of fools?

One of the most common criticisms of disaster movies is that they contain clichéd characters; stereotypes bordering on cardboard cut-outs. However, it could be argued that *Airport* was quite novel in deploying such clichéd characters so earnestly and that the criticism becomes much more

pertinent when the stereotypes themselves became such a common characteristic of disaster movies. If biblical epics also ran out of steam because
the worthy heroes and tyrannical villains could not carry the weight of the
glorious destruction around them, and science fiction B-movies ultimately
reached the point where audiences hoped that the clean-cut hero would
actually get fried by an alien death-ray, *Airport* came up with new combinations of reassuring stereotypes (the brave manager, the dashing pilot,
the cigar-munching engineer, the mad bomber, the nice little old lady) for
an entertaining streamlining of an old and pervasive genre (see Gertner
1970).

Like the business-like opening to the film, the characters are introduced
in suitably brisk ways. What marks *Airport* out from many of the other disaster movies that were to follow, however, is that most of the characters are
professionals who actually work for the airport and airline. As the disaster
cycle of the 1970s progressed, the public and passengers were to become
much more important, as disaster fodder to a certain extent but also fundamental to the requirement that ordinary folk were to be put under as much
extraordinary duress as possible. *Airport* dramatises the ways in which professionals can face up to, and ultimately succeed against, disaster. This
is not to say that the professionals are not themselves ordinary people
in extraordinary jobs, and the first recognisable conflict in this respect is
that between professional duty and personal commitments. This is clearly
established in the main star character, Mel Bakersfeld (Burt Lancaster), the
General Manager of the airport. Spending more time at work than at home,
the film makes it clear in a split-screen phone call from his wife, Cindy, that
the snowstorm will only confound the issue, as Bakersfeld has to miss an
important dinner with his wife's wealthy family. It also follows that because
he is spending so much time at work he is also spending more time with his
Customer Relations Officer, Tanya Livingstone (Jean Seberg). The fact that
Bakersfeld communicates with his wife and then children through split-
screen phone calls is clinically symbolic of the divide between job and
family, and the lack of interpersonal connection between husband and
wife. When Cindy visits the office the emergency narrative has become even
more pressing, further distinguishing the urgency of Bakersfeld's job from

his declining domestic situation. As he says to her when she first arrives: 'Why do you have to pick tonight to come out here and fight with me?' As it turns out, Cindy has her own emergency. The eldest daughter has gone to stay with her friends, despairing at the 'atmosphere of hate' between father and mother. Cindy's ultimatum is for them to give up their pretence and divorce. She calls him a 'bigamist' who is primarily married to his job and he emphasises that whereas his home life is 'important', the current emergency is much more 'imperative'. Cindy admits to having found another man ('someone who makes me feel wanted') and that conveniently lets Bakersfeld off the hook and free to approach Tanya. The conversation ends with Bakersfeld answering the phone and Cindy walking out of the office.

The other main relationship in *Airport* is the affair between Captain Vernon Demerest (Dean Martin) and his stewardess, Gwen Meighen (Jacqueline Bisset). It is immediately established that Demerest is Bakersfeld's brother-in-law, leading to plenty of initial antagonism between the go-getting pilot on a supervision run and the paper-shuffling manager who 'didn't always fly a desk'. The main difference in terms of the narrative action of the film, however, is that whereas Bakersfeld and Tanya are gradually brought together by the emergency on the ground, Demerest and Gwen are instantly brought closer together by the disaster in the air. At the beginning of the film Demerest is driven to the airport by his wife. As she relates to Bakersfeld, it is assumed that Demerest's fear of commitment to other women keeps him more or less faithful to her: as she significantly states, 'I'm his disaster insurance'. Having been driven from home to the airport, however, Demerest phones Gwen. When they meet up on the plane she reveals that she is pregnant and commitment becomes a very pressing issue. Having stopped taking the pill to avoid becoming overweight, while this might indicate that it was Gwen's fault, Demerest can only reply that he will pay for an abortion.

As far as the central disaster of the film is concerned, when the bomb goes off it kills the bomber and Gwen receives much of the impact. Decompression, battered passengers, cracking hull and spiralling plane aside, Gwen thus becomes a major focus. As the person receiving most of the blast, and with the captain's personal commitments brought to the fore (saving her and saving the plane), Gwen could be said to be the main victim of the film in two respects. On a personal level, this is due to Demerest's seeming lack of commitment, and, in terms of the action of the film, she is the main victim of the actual disaster. Demerest reveals to the doctor that she is pregnant, the co-captain offers his support and it becomes apparent that Demerest has finally committed himself to saving Gwen *and* the baby. Again, particularly in light of what was to follow in the 1970s disaster cycle, the co-pilot's observation of the passengers may seem only minimal: 'some cuts and bruises, shocks and puking'. Yet at root, however large the subsequent disasters, the personal stakes remain more or less the same.

Having taken control of the disaster in the air, Demerest is able to accompany Gwen to the hospital, sealing his commitment by holding her hand and saying: 'Hold on, you'll be alright. We're gonna make it'. And similarly, having solved the emergency on the ground, Bakersfeld is able to commit himself to going to Tanya's apartment and sampling her famous scrambled eggs. The film ends with their car leaving, planes lined up for more flights, and the airport positively glowing in the clear light of the next day. This is disaster as therapy, focusing the mind and helping you to decide what is really good for you. Disaster movies are thus not so much about clinging onto dear life as making your way, out of the rubble, towards a life with renewed perspective.

Camera politica

If disaster movies can be criticised for putting stock characters in standard, exceptional circumstances, as far as more in-depth analyses and criticisms of the genre are concerned, much attention has been directed towards the fact that these isolated stereotypes can also be read as offering a particular, microcosmic view of American society. This may well be the result of wanting to establish certain character types quickly and conveniently in order to get to the actual disasters as efficiently as possible, but in order for these characters to have an even more expedient resonance they are written and performed as representative types. The most trenchant analysis and critique of 1970s disaster movies in this respect is Michael Ryan and Douglas Kellner's *Camera Politica: The Politics and Ideology of Contemporary Hollywood Film* (1988). At root, Ryan and Kellner present disaster movies as unremittingly conservative:

> They exhibit a return to more traditional generic conventions and depict a society in crisis attempting to solve its social and cultural problems through the ritualized legitimation of strong male leadership, the renewal of traditional moral values, and the regeneration of institutions like the patriarchal family. (p. 23)

There may be something of a liberal twist in the way that these films also criticise 'unrestrained corporate capitalism' and 'the pursuit of profit' but such critique is usually moralistic, and the films 'advocate corporatist solutions whereby an elite of leaders, usually professionals or technocrats, enable groups of people to survive through coordinated, even obedient action' (p. 52).

Ryan and Kellner are at least open to the fact that this is 'usually' the case and they do go on to point out increasing deviations from the norm. However, given some of the more bitter and twisted disaster movies that were to follow, does this not leave *Airport* in even more of a time warp? Anything that gets in the way of the successful running of the airport is established as a nuisance, from the demonstrators protesting against noise levels, to the manager who wants to accede to their demands. On the plane, the nuisance passenger is almost as bad as the bomber who is unable to hold down a job and it is, in fact, the nuisance passenger's cowardly actions which lead to the bomber getting his briefcase back (ending with the bomber getting blown up and the passenger getting slapped by a priest). If such 'wimpish whining' can be read as 'democratic meddling' the film's 'rhetoric of class and sexuality' is even more strident:

> The airport manager's handicap is a rich wife who attempts to run his life. An anomaly in comparison to his decidedly more cooperative female sidekick, she is predictably dumped by the end of the film. The airport's salvation parallels liberation from her thrall, as it does

a decision by a stewardess not to get an abortion. Male sexual and social power, as much as an airplane, are at stake in the film, and middle-class family values prevail over the new sexual liberalism and over upper-class 'decadence'. (p. 53)

As Ryan and Kellner pointedly argue, 1970s disaster movies were 'markedly middle-aged, middle-level managerial, and mid-American' (p. 56). The middle-class ethos of *Airport* is firmly established in that decent, professional middle ground of sympathetic manager Bakersfeld and heroic captain Demerest. While Bakersfeld has to fight his 'upper-class' bosses over their decision to close the airport, Demerest has to fight the damage caused by a 'working-class' bomber who is after insurance money. If the main characters in the film are established as safely middle-class, and only slightly disturbed by domestic difficulties, the central disaster works in cutting through such minor calamities and clarifying their main aims in life:

> *Airport* closes with images of rejuvenation. It is sunny in the Midwest, and planes are landing safely. The troublesome protestors are gone, as is the troublesome worker. It is a golden moment for mid-American ideology. Corporations still look virtuous. The doubt, distrust, and scepticism that will characterize the seventies have yet to set in. Few later disaster films match the arrogance of this vision of American hope. (p. 53)

Class wars

By way of slightly refining Ryan and Kellner's forceful account, it is helpful to focus on the bomber D. O. Guerrero (Van Heflin) and the chief engineer Jo Patroni (George Kennedy). For Ryan and Kellner, Guerrero is central to the literal class warfare of *Airport*, but it can be argued that he is presented much more sympathetically than their blanket ideological account suggests. Certainly, there is a great difference between the ways in which respective lifestyles are represented in the film:

It constructs a world of people at home with cocktail lounge Muzac, repressed sexuality, nice little old ladies, fireplace warmth, soap-opera décor, and moral oppositions instantiated in the difference between bright, unshadowed lighting in middle-class settings and underground darkness in working-class settings, where music from fifties horror films codes the world as one to be feared. (Ryan and Keller 1988: 53)

This contrast does become apparent when we first see Guerrero in his dark, dank apartment. With ominous music in the background and a close-up of the explosive content of Guerrero's briefcase, the message is simple enough. What is particularly interesting about this 'mad bomber' figure, however, is that he goes on to be presented as a relatively complex and often sympathetic character. More time is spent on Guerrero's character, in fact, than the sketchy plane passengers. If a 'mad' bomber, he is at least a well-rounded mad bomber, and it could be said that there is as much interest as to whether he will explode the bomb and what *his* fate will be. So, after the initial dread, the film spends much more time in fleshing out his family life and background psychology. Guerrero's wife Inez (Maureen Stapleton) is presented as one of the most sympathetic characters in the entire film. In contrast to the petty foibles of the rich and their throwaway marriages, the Guerreros try to scrape a decent living so that they can stay together. With Guerrero out of work and Inez working at the diner, all that they need is enough money to live on, and it becomes clear that while Guerrero may well be planning a rather extreme insurance fraud, for him it is the only decent thing to do: 'I haven't been a very good provider but I will be, I promise'.

Whilst adding to the necessary tension, Inez's race to stop her husband before he gets on the plane also provides an extra, personal channel of sympathy for the audience. This may be assuming too much because, ultimately, audiences go to watch disaster movies to watch disasters. However, Ryan and Kellner neglect the fact that that not all of the cinema-going audiences of the time will have been middle class. A very specific definition of the middle class is inherent in their reading of the film: that increasing sector of American society in the 1970s earning between $15,000 and $40,000 per year. Whether looked at from the perspective of increasingly marginal working-class audiences enjoying disaster being delivered upon the middle-class majority, or middle-class audiences enjoying watching the rich and famous being put under as much duress as possible, the sadistic side of disaster movies is rarely balanced by sympathy. Characters are so swiftly sketched and despatched that only the outsiders literally stand out. The details follow, for example, that Guerrero is part Irish and part Spanish, and as Inez eventually reveals to Bakersfeld, behind the poverty we also find out that Guerrero's problems began as a demolition expert in the army. Shell-shocked, put into an army hospital and unable to control himself under similar situations, the cause and effect are such that Guerrero cannot follow his expertise through to excavation work because that prior expertise is part of his mental problem. Far from marking him out as lazy, or as a man who quite simply cannot hold down a job, such background psychology moves the emphasis away from working-class weakness and belligerence (as Ryan and Kellner ultimately suggest) towards an attempt at addressing the failure of state care.

If Ryan and Kellner tend to present Guerrero as a working-class villain, what they appear to forget is that the film also has a working-class hero. They are probably right in seeing Patroni as a symbol of masculine authority, 'defying effeminate experts and proper procedures alike' in his efforts to clear the runway (p. 53), but what they ignore is that, in contrast to the philandering, smartly dressed Bakersfeld and Demerest, Patroni is a much more down-to-earth hero, an 'ordinary Jo' safe enough in his marriage to get on with the job at hand. When he is called away from his wife (he is the only character in the film we see happily married) it is because he is the right man for the wrong situations: 'They don't call it an emergency anymore, they call it a Patroni'. As if his surname was not enough to follow 'ordinary Jo' through to connotations of 'patron' and 'patrol', when he arrives at the scene he chews on his characteristic cigar, puts his TWA baseball cap on and thoroughly motivates the tired maintenance team. If Patroni does represent masculine authority, in contrast to democratic whingers and ineffectual pen pushers, the point is that he does his job and does not take orders. In portraying Patroni as an expert in his field rather than a worker under command, his 'working' relationship with Bakersfeld is presented in an overly positive light. Both of these characters have an airforce background and, following on from the scene in which Bakersfeld squares up to the airport executives, this common-sense manager allows Patroni to work his way around restrictive plane regulations. Cutting through the paperwork in such a way, the film itself works in cutting through a class distinction based on bureaucracy at the top and taking orders down below with mutual respect. When Patroni succeeds in clearing the runway, the fusion of man and machine (actual physical work) is explicitly set against bureaucratic rules and regulations. 'The instruction book said that was impossible,' says one of his co-workers. Patroni replies: 'Ah, there's one nice thing about the 707. It can do anything but read'. There is one line, following on from this, that Ryan and Kellner regard as very telling. When the co-pilot looks at the plane, he shows his admiration for the corporate aspect of the machine by saying: 'Remind me to send a thank-you note to Mr. Boeing'. Emphasising this line and ignoring the former is symptomatic of Ryan and Kellner's account of the film. In its celebration of 'both traditional individualism and the new corporatism' (p. 52), the odds are against *Airport* making clear, radical statements.

The spawn of Airport

Particularly in light of the new, alternative, film-making that had begun to transform Hollywood in the late 1960s (for example *Bonnie and Clyde* (1967) and *Easy Rider* (1969)), *Airport* has always been regarded as old-fashioned. Judith Crist recognised as much at the time by calling it 'the best film of 1944' (quoted in Walker 2000: 12). Similarly, with its emphasis on character and emergency rather than hardcore disaster, in contrast to the disaster movies that were to follow in its wake, *Airport* is as leisurely as an airport lounge. The most successful disaster movies of the 1970s were the ones that paid more or less equal attention to character and disaster, the compromise being that the characters developed through the action. If *The Poseidon Adventure*, *The Towering Inferno* and, to a certain extent,

Earthquake were the best of the cycle in this respect, *Airport* featured minimal disaster and its subsequent series far too little characterisation. Although beginning promisingly, with the pilots incapacitated and the stewardess (Karen Black) taking control of the plane, *Airport 1975* spends far too much time on its improbable mid-air rescue, and then Charlton Heston takes over. The last of the series, *The Concorde – Airport '79*, did at least try to update proceedings by featuring the latest streamlined plane, and changed the formula slightly by featuring some sort of corporate conspiracy element. However, both of these factors count for little when all that Captain Patroni has to do to avert the disaster is divert heat-seeking missiles with a flare gun.

Airport '77 illustrates the most symptomatic differences and developments. The differences are such that whereas in *Airport* the main plane takes off after 70 minutes, in *Airport '77* it takes off in less than 15. *Airport '77* is an *Airport* film without an airport and duly proceeds with the action at a much quicker pace. Here the plane crashes into the ocean within 40 minutes, in contrast to the bomb exploding 30 minutes from the end in the original *Airport*. Following on from the discussion about Guerrero, what is particularly noticeable is that the subsequent *Airport* films completely depersonalise the human causes of disaster. Located in-between the pilot unfit to fly his jet in *Airport 1975* and the scheming saboteurs of *Airport '79*, *Airport '77* centres on a group of professional art thieves. The progression is such that while Guerrero is given a range of sympathetic motives, here the villains are just faceless criminals. Direct continuity is maintained by featuring Patroni as a recurring figure throughout the series. By *Airport '77*, however, he is an altogether different character, merely acting as a liaison between the airline and the naval rescue team. He has been promoted and, in the process, is completely stripped of his previous working-class affinities. Stuck in the operations room and mostly talking on the radio, he no longer gets his hands dirty and cannot even chew on his cigar any more. He becomes a literal mouthpiece in terms of the plot (advising on the action from afar) and for the corporation, here represented by the kind old figure of James Stewart (who is dying of cancer and wants to see his grandchildren before he dies). The former working-class hero, Patroni, thus ends up reassuring his friend, the paternal figure behind the steely corporation, 'Don't worry, Phil, we'll get that plane up, and in one piece'.

So, with no working-class affinities and little meddling bureaucracy, what remains? Captain Gallagher is a good combination of Demerest and Patroni, a pilot who gets his hands dirty and, as played by Jack Lemmon, is thoroughly reasonable. Yet his character comes to nought when the final quarter of the film is entirely devoted to the actions of the Navy bringing the plane to the surface. All that remains is a group of rather unsympathetic characters privileged enough to be on this exclusive 'dream machine' and with their riches stored in the cargo hold. The subsequent *Airport* series gets down to the character deficient and most repetitive action essentials of the 1970s disaster cycle – a certain distance and relish in watching the rich (the characters) and famous (the stars) beset by disaster.

The Poseidon Adventure

The three most strident and successful disaster movies of the 1970s were *The Poseidon Adventure*, *The Towering Inferno* and *Earthquake*. As Maurice Yacowar's classifications continue, these films clearly take us from 'The Ship of Fools' to 'The City Fails'. In the first instance, *The Poseidon Adventure* presents us with a very literal ship of fools scenario where the passengers could be said to be taken to task for the mere hubris of attempting to float (or, if God had intended us to swim he would have given us fins). *Titanic* (1953) and *A Night to Remember* (1958) are the most obvious historical precedents in this respect. Then, after the transport problems of *Airport* and *The Poseidon Adventure*, *The Towering Inferno* and *Earthquake* take us into the next, more landlocked but equally hubristic category of 'The City Fails': 'Here man is most dramatically punished for placing his faith in his own works and losing sight of his maker. So his edifices must crumble about him' (Yacowar 1977: 92–3). This category stretches from the ancient past of *The Last Days of Pompeii* to the futuristic *Metropolis* (1926).

If we can look back on *Airport* as providing a certain template, Nick Roddick correctly asserts that it was *The Poseidon Adventure* that confidently cranked up the spectacular disaster and consequently provided for much more peril and a massive death toll. As an impetus for approaching the pumped-up spectacle and sheer carnage of what was to follow, Roddick uses producer Irwin Allen's words in order to establish the basic industrial formula:

> We have a perfect set-up of a group of people who have never met before and who are thrown together in terrible circumstances. In the first six minutes, 1,400 people are killed and only the stars survive. (Quoted in Roddick 1980: 243)

There are qualifications to be made to this pitch, but for now it does get to the grisly heart of the matter: stars and character actors randomly thrown together and put under more duress than they can stand, the disasters more elaborate than ever and the fatalities extreme. So, while certain factors – such as the elements and increasing reliance upon dependable (and often recurring) star names – provide for continuity throughout the 1970s disaster cycle as a whole, it is first worth looking at the ways in which *The Poseidon Adventure* actually differs from *Airport* by way of understanding the subsequent developments.

In terms of the potential death rate, the SS Poseidon holds far more passengers and crew than the Golden Argosy. There is a certain parallel to be maintained with the combined airport and airplane drama of *Airport*, in the sense that just as the airport establishes a huge amount of potential victims and dwindles them down to an aisle's worth on the plane, the purser describes the Poseidon as 'a hotel with a bow and a stern stuck on' and the film similarly focuses on a particular group in peril. The main difference, however, is that while *Airport* gets down to its core group by the very nature of them becoming passengers (leaving the relative safety of the airport behind), *The Poseidon Adventure* gets down to its core of passengers by wiping out a thousand others in the main flood. In terms of the beginning of these films, similarly the sea storm could be said to provide as much an indication of the bigger, sub-sea earthquake waves that would follow as the snowstorm and its consequent problems in *Airport*. But the disaster that hits the Poseidon is far greater than that which befalls Demerest's plane. If the Poseidon can just about manage the tidal waves at the beginning of the film, the main impact wave 20 minutes later is much larger and the ship is unable to withstand such force.

In terms of the relative transport, actually there is at first little indication that the Poseidon is a luxurious ship. In contrast to the gleaming, busy airport or the glossy new plane in *Airport*, the few passengers that we see on the decks of the Poseidon are cold and weathered, the cinematography is grainy and the cockpit looks very old-fashioned indeed. As Captain Harrison (Leslie Neilsen) states, this is an old ship and cannot take the extra cargo and full speed ahead as demanded by the owner's representative, Linarcos. Similarly, when we are introduced to the main passengers their cabins look quite modest. The grand old opulence of the ship is finally revealed to us, however, when the passengers enter the ballroom in order to take part in New Year celebrations. This is the centre of luxury and what duly follows is that it becomes the scene of the central, spectacular disaster.

The main wave hits and the ballroom is over-turned with the ship, the guests smashing into glass partitions, the Christmas tree falling down and with some of the passengers left stuck on tables hanging from the ceiling. Which is to say that this impressive and presumably expensive set is used to its fullest, providing for the film's centrepiece sequence. Contrast this with the much more limited explosion in *Airport* and the greater scale of the disaster in *The Poseidon Adventure* becomes even more apparent.

At root, then, we could say that subsequent disaster movies differed from *Airport* in terms of sheer violent spectacle. Allied to the greater size of the disasters, however, we also have a greater degree of isolation. While the opening storm of *The Poseidon Adventure* partly echoes the snowstorm in *Airport*, the passengers and crew of the Poseidon are literally all at sea from the offset, completely cut off from the outside world. What we need to remember about the snowstorm in *Airport* is that it provides for emergency rather than disaster. It may well isolate Lincoln Airport, but the airport is a relatively self-sufficient base the size of a small town and retains landlocked communication with the plane (the real focus of the disaster) throughout. The odds of surviving a dip in the sea may well be higher than falling from the sky, but the Poseidon's only connection with the outside world is through the radio announcement that a huge tidal wave is on its way. What makes the situation even worse is that the captain and principal cabin crew are the first to die from the impact, leaving the passengers in an even more isolated and rudderless state. At least, in *Airport*, Demerest and his co-pilots are able to guide their damaged plane by communicating with ground control, and with Bakersfeld and Patroni actively working to clear the runway. In *The Poseidon Adventure* the passengers are left to fend almost entirely for themselves, with the main group making its way up to the propeller shaft in the uncertain hope that they will be spotted and rescued on the surface of the over-turned ship. Apart from the steward, Acres (Roddy McDowall), who is partly able to guide the group until he dies, the only other remaining crewmembers are, in fact, a nuisance. The ship's doctor may mistakenly lead another group the wrong way but, in holding the majority of the passengers back, the purser is at least partly responsible for hundreds of deaths. As well as the enormity of the disaster, therefore, *The Poseidon Adventure* subsequently presents us with extremely hazardous attempts at survival, the ship all at sea, upside down and with the main group left fighting for (and often amongst) themselves.

Survival and salvation

With the ship already in the middle of the ocean, in the first pre-disaster phase of *The Poseidon Adventure*, we are also introduced to the characters with less detail about their home lives. Whereas we actually see the homes and family lives of many of the principal characters in *Airport*, in *The Poseidon Adventure* 'home' is very much a sketchy background and 'land' is the key hope. This impacts enormously on any conventional class readings that can be brought to bear on the film. Class, or more precisely class perception, does become a particular issue in relation to Rogo (Ernest Borgnine) and his wife Linda (Stella Stevens). As they get ready for dinner at the captain's table, it becomes clear that they are not used to such refined gatherings. He is a jobbing cop and she an ex-prostitute afraid that she might get recognised by one of her former clients. But it is not so much class difference that becomes an issue throughout the film as Rogo's diffidence, unwilling to take blind orders from their self-appointed leader, unable to take charge himself and not sure whether he should join another group. He is a would-be man of action who becomes a complainer and has to adapt to this altogether different, lawless situation.

With the class distinctions eroded to the level of personality traits, the main ideological focus of the film is provided by religion. With a ship called the Poseidon travelling from modern-day New York to ancient Athens, the mythological connotations are obvious. The references may well be as much to biblical epics as the Bible itself, but even the smallest details become significant when located in this wider context of the ancient and the modern. The Rosens (Shelley Winters and Jack Albertson), for example, want to stop off in Israel, mostly to visit their granddaughter but also to see the holy Moses sites as advertised in their tourist brochure. As far as the narrative is concerned, the sub-sea earthquake originating in Crete may well be a mere plot device (it had to originate somewhere) but, with the wider theme of hubris in mind, all of these modern-day commercial travellers are also being tested, even punished, by an act of God. If Moses provides us with one reference to hazardous but ultimately safe navigation of the sea, Poseidon is the obvious counterpoint. As the captain explains, when Linda enquires about the ship's main ornamental statue: 'The great god Poseidon. In Greek mythology the god of the sea, also god of storms, tempests, earthquakes and other natural disasters. Quite an ill-tempered fellow'. When this is followed by an emergency red light drawing the captain to the bridge, it becomes clear that Poseidon is feeling particularly ill-tempered that day, possibly even insulted by the captain's description of him. With the main tidal wave approaching, the captain can only say: 'Oh my God!', and similarly, after the wave has hit, one of the passengers can only ask: 'Jesus Christ, what happened?'

The Poseidon Adventure is packed with people taking the Lord's name in vain.

If these are all accumulating and, it must be said, increasingly indiscriminate nods towards Greek/Christian mythology and the wrath of God/gods, Reverend Scott (Gene Hackman) provides the most specific response to the fateful power of religion. This self-styled turbulent priest preaches the one in the whole rather than the whole in the one, imploring his flock to 'Pray to that part of God within you' and to become active 'winners' rather than remaining passive 'quitters'. When the disaster hits, Scott duly leaps into action rather than praying for salvation, significantly leading his group up the fallen Christmas tree. While the purser positively defies Scott, the ship's chaplain (Arthur O'Connell) stays behind to tend the wounded and rightly points out that Scott is only preaching to 'the strong'. The two men of the cloth do respect each other's opinions, and affectionately part, but then the passive, fatalistic majority is wiped out as the ballroom suddenly floods. In the central disaster of the film, the image of a benevolent God is completely overturned by the act of a vengeful God and the passive belief in salvation is completely taken to task. But what of Scott's own, alternative ideology? The film is not afraid to question blind faith in the orthodox or the unorthodox. Scott is presented as angry, belligerent and even messianic. Rogo may well complain too much but astutely asks, 'Who do you think you are, God Himself?' Scott does lead the group towards the main exit but not without casualties along the way. When Linda falls to her death Rogo turns to the group's 'god' and shouts, 'I started to believe in your promises ... You took from me the only thing I loved in the entire world ... you killed her!' All of which leads Scott to commit the ultimate self-sacrifice. Jumping to a heated valve, he rails against God: 'How many more sacrifices? How much more blood? How many more lives? Beryl wasn't enough, then Acres, now the girl. You want another life then take me!' Having managed to turn the valve that opens the door, he can only hang there and then drop into the burning fire below. The sacrifice is made and the baton of responsibility passed from priest to policeman. James Martin (Red Buttons) makes the lesson clear to Rogo: 'What kind of a policeman are you? You've done nothing but beef and complain, always negative, always destructive. Well now's your chance to do something positive for a change. Are you quitting, Mr Rogo? Going down with a whimper, on your belly?' Rogo rises to the task and leads the five remaining survivors up into safety.

Industry and ideology

The poster for *The Poseidon Adventure* has a great tagline that gets straight to the point: 'Hell. Upside Down'. The film deploys its mythic, moral symbolism with a wrench, but what better way to rid a turbulent priest than have him fall into nothing less than the burning fire of an upside-down, boiler room hell? As Nick Roddick states in relation to the 1970s disaster cycle as a whole:

> If *The Poseidon Adventure* is more or less alone in making explicit use of religious imagery, the idea of the disaster as a primitive elemental test sent by God is strongly present in all the movies with the exception of *Juggernaut*. What is more ... a recurring image in the movies is that of the rescuer appearing from on high like an angel. (1980: 254)

Given the particular, explicit nature of *The Poseidon Adventure*, the final image is, indeed, a welcome corrective to all the previous deluge and damnation as the hull door opens and the Navy appears, the survivors boarding a helicopter and ascending into the sky. Subsequent ideological readings cut through the eternal moralising and get down to context. As Ryan and Kellner continue after their reading of *Airport*, for example:

> As the crisis in confidence intensified during the seventies, more was needed than a tough maintenance man to clear the runways. At this time, many people began turning to evangelical religion and born-again Christianity for relief from a world of disappointment, insecurity, and frustration that inflation and unemployment helped usher in. (1988: 54–5)

FIGURE 2 *The Poseidon Adventure: A Test of Leadership*

Moving away from their trenchant critique of the shiny corporate optimism of *Airport*, Ryan and Kellner go on to follow the ways in which the 1970s disaster cycle did become much less idealistic. But, in light of the increasing disasters, they argue a tightening rather than loosening of the reins of ideology. Their reading of *The Poseidon Adventure* thus follows in terms of 'right-wing, religiously based authoritarian solutions' (p. 54).

It can be argued that the more bitter and twisted the disasters throughout the 1970s, the more solutions are tested to their limits in these films. For example, Scott has to die because he rails against God; conversely, he is, in fact, proven right in refusing to accept the herd instinct and gather his flock his own way. Depending on which view is taken, his death can be read as thoroughly deserved or a defiant act of supreme self-sacrifice. On a more structural level, it is interesting that in *The Poseidon Adventure* the 'only the stars survive' formula is stretched to breaking point. In a sense, the ideal disaster movie would be one that satisfies innate industrial demands and subsequent ideological readings by having its stars play the morally upright characters and its character actors the greedy and cowardly ones. In one fell swoop, the heroic stars survive and the rest get what they deserve. Yet it does not work that way with this film. By way of testing the relative demands of the industrial and ideological, therefore, it is worth considering the hierarchical cast list of *The Poseidon Adventure*. The poster for the film splits the eleven main characters into seven stars and four co-stars. Whether we look at the seven stars in terms of their own hierarchy or consider them all as a veritable ensemble, the list proceeds as follows: Gene Hackman, Ernest Borgnine, Red Buttons, Carol Lynley, Roddy McDowall, Stella Stevens, Shelley Winters. From a very clinical, statistical perspective, cutting through to the essential rates of death and survival with a sharp, industrial scalpel, by the end of the film four of these stars are dead. Following on from this crumbling hierarchy, the four co-stars are Jack Albertson, Pamela Sue Martin (Susan), Arthur O'Connell and Eric Shea (Robin), only one of whom actually dies.

Even if we were to cut the ensemble of stars down to the first two, the main problem is still the fact that the leading star, Gene Hackman, does not survive. From an ideological perspective one might have at least expected the weak and belligerent Rogo to die instead, but if this seems too clinical a judgement, consider Ryan and Kellner's one-line summary of the group's main progress: 'They undergo numerous tests, and the weak (two women, most notably) fall by the wayside' (1988: 54). If Scott and Rogo can be regarded the strongest characters and the rest weak, why is it that most of the weak also survive Scott? Similarly, more men die than women, and as many women survive as do not, why this casual link between the weak and the women? The fact is that the more such ideological readings follow the same pattern of the survival of the fittest, the exceptions in the films become much more significant than the assumed generic rules. Ryan and Kellner do admit that *The Poseidon Adventure* is 'the first disaster film to sympathetically incorporate young people' (p. 54). But while this, too, can be followed through to its conservative ideological connotations (young people need the most guid-ance), the more practical, industrial reasoning is that Hollywood cinema needed to widen its demographics and sacrificing the women, teenagers and children would have proven far too alienating.

The Towering Inferno

The industrial readings of the 1970s disaster cycle are such that the disasters and characters in the films themselves result out of the combined draw of spectacle and stars, the ideal being that the stars are as spectacular a draw as the spectacular disasters. With regard to this element of the genre, *The Towering Inferno* is quite possibly the most impressive of all disaster movies, not only in terms of the 1970s but also in comparison with more recent standards – as evidenced in a film like *Backdraft* (1991), for example. Model and matte shots stand up well (with enough fire and smoke to disguise the miniatures and enhance the perceived scale) but the set pieces are particularly well-staged, with both stuntmen and stars right in the heart of the perilous action. The fire highlights are obvious enough – the first backdraft, Robert Wagner and Susan Flannery stuck in their office trying to get out, the creeping flames and sudden explosions – but air and water also get in the way, simultaneously feeding and starving the fire. Gravity is a peril – from Paul Newman traversing the crippled stairs, to the scenic elevator coming unstuck from the side of the building (and water ineffectual until it becomes a dangerous deluge) – the last solution being to explode the rooftop water tanks and violently flood the promenade room. Individual stunts are particularly well-staged and often grisly, but the main contrast is that, whereas today stars might face up to a blue screen for computer-generated effects to be added later, this and the other main disaster movies of the time really put their stars under pressure. As if all of that water was not enough to almost drown *The Poseidon Adventure* cast (the film was shot in sequence exactly so that the actors would look more haggard as the film progressed), there are particular close-ups of Paul Newman and poor old Fred Astaire when the water tanks explode that make watching *The Towering Inferno* a real peril and a curious pleasure. The ideological readings are such that we go to see these films to watch the rich and greedy get their comeuppance; an allied draw is watching famous film stars really working for their money.

The Towering Inferno is also the most star-studded disaster movie, the point being that star power really does live up to the power of its spectacle. As Nick Roddick explains, the basic use of stars in disaster movies, the narrative compression of a random gathering of people is further facilitated by pre-existing star personas. The narratives themselves call for ensemble casting and particular actors bring instant recognition:

> Disaster movies are peopled by archetypes who react to the given situation in function of their sex, class or profession and not in function of any individual identity. What is more, the archetypes are extended by the known personality of the star playing the part: in accordance with the usual formula, what we respond to on the screen is not someone called Stuart Graff (*Earthquake*) or Alan Murdock (*Airport 1975*), but someone far more substantial called Charlton Heston. (1980: 252)

Yacowar also follows the same economy through to *The Towering Inferno*: 'An inherited sentiment plays around Jennifer Jones and Fred Astaire, Robert Vaughn repeats his corrupt politician from *Bullitt*, and Richard Chamberlain reprises his corrupt All-American from *Petulia*, itself an ironic inversion of his Kildare' (1977: 97). The problem with both of these readings, however, is that they are based on conservative assumptions, principally that stars known for playing heroic types will go on to do the same in disaster movies. In line with Roddick's star survival argument, Charlton Heston plays Charlton Heston and the implications are that we can expect him to rescue the *Airport 1975* plane as confidently as he rode his chariot in *Ben-Hur*. In this case he does and that is extremely reassuring. An opposite attraction of disaster movies, however, is that sometimes the stars do not survive. They may die heroically and the films might well play on the usual expectations exactly in order to create the opposite effect, but the twist is that not even star images set in stone can survive disaster. So while it might have been entirely appropriate to have the rock-like, chisel-jawed Charlton Heston face up to *Earthquake*, it was an unexpected pleasure to see the man who parted the Red Sea in *The*

Ten Commandments get washed down the drain at the end of the film. Yacowar's list is interesting in that it does establish *The Towering Inferno*'s clever mix of old and new Hollywood stars. The 'inherited sentiment' of Fred Astaire and Jennifer Jones is certainly used playfully and both the creepy Vaughn and weasly Chamberlain do get their comeuppance. Not all of the corrupt characters in the film die, but part of the wonderful predictability is that we cannot wait for these two characters, at least, to get what they deserve. But how will Fred Astaire and Jennifer Jones fare? The most accomplished disaster movies remain true to the indiscriminate nature of disaster, both fulfilling and shattering our expectations and illusions.

In terms of both form and its principal use of stars, *The Towering Inferno* is actually one of the most reassuring disaster movies of the 1970s. Look at the neat composition of the poster, for example, the cast on the left and the towering inferno on the right (see figure 3). The compromise of the two most prominent faces was to put Steve McQueen to the left, but slightly lower than Paul Newman, with Newman's name first (here top and central) in credit listings. Combined, their heads are bigger than the skyscraper, and note the way in which all of the faces in the poster are given character types – The Architect, The Fire Chief, The Builder, The Girlfriend, The Con Man, The Wife, The Son-in-Law, The Widower, The Security Man, The Senator, The Publicity Man. Boxed in and given labels, why not play the Disaster Movie game from the comfort of your own queue. Who do you expect to survive? What is particularly interesting with regard to these character types are the ways in which the men are primarily defined in relation to their jobs and the women are defined solely in terms of their relationships with men. A class-based reading of *The Towering Inferno* would seize upon the opportunity afforded by arranging the 'bread-winners' into a hierarchy, ranging from The Security Man (O. J. Simpson) at the bottom to The Senator (Robert Vaughn) at the top. Of principal interest, however, are those in the centre, the characteristic 'middle ground' of disaster movies. Hence the primary class conflict in the film is that developed between the 'professionals', The Architect (Paul Newman) and The Fire Chief (Steve McQueen), and the 'money men',

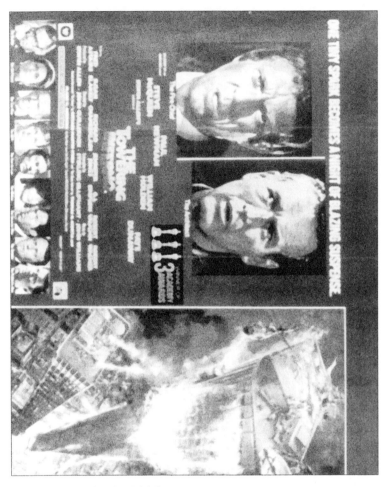

FIGURE 3 *The Towering Inferno: Stars in their Element*

The Builder (William Holden) and his Son-In-Law (Richard Chamberlain). A gendered — or more precisely, feminist — reading of the film would quite rightly point out that the female characters are caught in a socially defined life cycle. The women represent a very literal 'progression' in this respect: the relatively independent Girlfriend (Faye Dunaway), the loyal

Wife (Susan Blakely) and the lonely Widow (Jennifer Jones). Where this might well point to a masculine bias in disaster movies of the period (which, as we have seen, is also reflected in *Airport* and *The Poseidon Adventure*), it could be argued that all characters are restricted in some way, principally the men defined in terms of roles and the women defined in terms of relationships. This is part of the shorthand required for squeezing a range of characters into disaster-driven situations and the stereotypes available at the time. Thus, star personas become even more important in this respect, in the sense that while the characters and their fates are fundamentally determined by the script, their development and our attitudes towards them are further informed by sheer casting.

The most specific analysis of the use of stars in *The Towering Inferno* is provided by Richard Dyer, in what could well be the first example of his formative interest in 'Star Studies' (Dyer 1975 and 1998). Dyer begins by looking at the reassuring nature of the film's composition. In contrast to the dirty, grainy, shaky *Poseidon Adventure* and *Earthquake*, *The Towering Inferno* is shot with clear and striking visuals. This is not to dismiss the film as clinical in form or predictable in its subsequent narrative, rather to explain that it stood out from an increasingly cluttered genre. Its clarity makes its action and disaster scenes all the more shocking and exciting, and a further reason for the film's popularity was its equally distinct use of stars. As Dyer continues, using Fred Astaire and Jennifer Jones to portray a twilight romance is, indeed, particularly affecting; similarly in the modern casting, Faye Dunaway gives 'a sensuality and a strength' to her role which distinguishes her character from the usual disaster movie bias of cloying wives and screaming girlfriends. Part of the film's 'reassuring' nature, however, is that while Dunaway brings a certain strength to her role, Paul Newman and Steve McQueen bring even more strength to their much more central roles. Dyer argues that the casting of Newman and McQueen is the film's 'master-stroke'. In a movie that privileges action and reaction over complex characterisations, it is principally their piercing blue eyes that mark them out as dependable, unflinching and heroic:

Those eyes are a feature of Newman and McQueen's images, but meaningfully exchanged looks between men are an important element in the narrative of *The Towering Inferno*. Several of the incidents … end with two men looking hard and trustingly at each other – they've come through something perilous together and survived through mutual dependence. Looking square and silent at each other is a model of transparency and trust between males (it is a mode deriving from westerns, and particularly dwelt on in spaghetti westerns). (1975: 31–2)

Two points that Dyer does not expressly follow are, firstly, these stars' wider images and, secondly, further connotations in their blue eyes. As the reference to westerns partly suggests, stars also bring with them reassuring signs from other genres (Charlton Heston being a good case in point). Newman and McQueen have starred in contemporary inflections on the western but, as respective roles in *Cool Hand Luke* (1967) and as 'the Cooler King' in *The Great Escape* (1963) further indicate, these two are the kings of cool united in a film full of heat. Dyer does refer to the 'cool and dark' look of *The Towering Inferno*'s modern interiors, gradually overwhelmed by the 'yellows and reds' of the fire (pp. 32–3), but even more so consider the cool, liquid property of blue. Fred Astaire has blue eyes but they are old and watery. Newman and McQueen have icy, piercing, steely stares, and only they can face up to the flaming disaster ahead.

There is, however, an equally effective divergence when it comes to the other stars and co-stars in *The Towering Inferno*. It could be said that Astaire's past image is much stronger than his character in determining his fate in the film. The previously light-footed Astaire plays a light-fingered con man. With such a dubious character, lying his way into the opening night so that he can fleece rich widows, you would expect the disaster to make him pay. Particularly bearing in mind that he begins by picking on the perfectly nice Jennifer Jones, why is it that Astaire survives and this poor old widow, having helped rescue her grandchildren and the family cat, falls to her death? While we are in the clinical business of playing the Disaster Movie game and assessing the relative worth of the characters, why should the gracious Jennifer Jones die and William Holden live? Holden is just as responsible for the disaster as his son-in-law, leading Chamberlain into cutting construction costs and getting to deliver the classic, fatal disaster movie line when Newman comes to him with a burnt-out wire at the beginning of the film: 'I think you're over-reacting'. Strengthening the question even further, why should the innocent Jennifer Jones die and the man who is at least partly responsible for her death live? The compromise option is one that levels all readings of the moral melting pot of disaster movies: redemption. The point about Astaire is that he falls in love with Jones, admits his sins to her and has to pay when his new-found love dies. That is, he becomes a better person because of her and because of her death. For his part, Holden survives exactly so that he can go on to build a better, safer world. Newman might well survive to design safer buildings, with McQueen always there for health and safety advice, but Holden is the sort of man who will go on to provide the money. As he says to his grieving daughter: 'All I can do now is pray to God that I can stop this from ever happening again'. Disaster movies do not always play fair but even in death there are life lessons to be learned. It's all in the stars. Only the repentant survive.

The end of the beginning

Disaster movies became increasingly redundant as the 1970s progressed. On a basic generic level it could be said that disaster movies of the period became increasingly limited by their own ostensible realism, the cycle having quickly reached its ideal balance of believability and extravagance with *The Towering Inferno* and *Earthquake* in 1974. The *Airport* series did provide suitably retrograde continuity throughout the 1970s, but anything much more than an earthquake would have sent disaster movies into sheer extravagance and, in the case of *Meteor* (1979) at least, a totally different genre. So if part of the attraction of the disaster movie cycle of the 1970s is that it began just one step ahead of the audience's fears, its progression and decline were one and the same thing. The other problem with the cycle is that, as the disasters did become more and more spectacular, the same representative characters remained in the same narrative situations. But seen from these simple generic perspectives, how could disaster movies possibly develop? Any more disaster would make them ludicrous fantasies and any more character would make them completely different, as if the only way to confront disaster or the development of disaster was to hold onto sheer, comforting familiarity. The only way forward, it would seem, was to follow *The Big Bus* route through to *Airplane* (1980). Replace the mad bomber with food poisoning and the disaster is easier to laugh at: follow the attempts of an ex-pilot with a drink problem trying to land a plane full of hysterical passengers and laugh at the ways in which the genre used to take itself so seriously.

The Hollywood film industry certainly found itself transformed by the end of the decade, to the extent that disaster movies can now be looked back on as little more than a box-office fad. This is not to dismiss the disaster cycle of the 1970s but to point out that, actually, disaster movies were there at the beginning of what has come to be known as the 'New Hollywood' and can well be regarded as the first successful genre in an industry that has become most notable for producing films according to generic fashions. Having been in operation for over thirty years, the New Hollywood has developed through numerous stages (see, for example, Schatz 1993; Smith 1998; Cook & Bernink 1999). Located between breakthrough films of the late 1960s and the supercharged blockbusting wave instigated by *Jaws* and *Star Wars* (1977), disaster movies of the early to mid-1970s can be regarded as transitional in several important respects. While the 'alternative' success of films like *Bonnie and Clyde* and *Easy Rider* had led the American film industry to reconsider some of it more mainstream studio practices, nevertheless by 1974 'the box-office returns of big-budget "multiple jeopardy" films ... again put corporate Hollywood in the expansive mood' (Madsen 1975: 160–1). Thus shake-up was followed by over-consolidation. If *Bonnie and Clyde* and *Easy Rider* can be said to have spoken to a new generation disaffected by Vietnam and the increasingly mythical American way of life, big stars and big explosions brought parents and teens back to the cinema soon after (see Kaplan 1975). However contradictory the evidence – their critique of corporate greed and cluttering up their extravagant sets with all sorts of mangled remains – disaster movies of the time were edgy but ultimately reassuring, violent but thoroughly spectacular, expensive but most of all profitable. That the New Hollywood was to quickly move on to other more profitable genres in the mid- to late 1970s, however, goes some way to illustrating that while disaster movies had taught the industry some valuable lessons, chief among them it would seem, was to strike while the iron was hot and then let things cool down. Disaster movies would not re-emerge, in concentrated form, until the 1990s. Recognisable elements of disaster movies did, however, feature in a new wave of action movies from the late 1980s into the 1990s, providing for further transitional developments in an ongoing history of disaster and survival.

2   TRANSITIONS: ACTION AND DISASTER

Beginning in the late 1970s, the singular void left by disaster movies would be filled by a wave of 'action-adventure' films which went on to constitute a dominant trend in contemporary Hollywood cinema. Action and science fiction blockbusters, in particular, have provided much-needed relief from the pervasive themes of 'disintegration and breakdown' (Wood 1986: 1986) that had progressively characterised both alternative and mainstream film-making from the mid-1960s to the mid-1970s. From the late 1970s to the present day, subsequent cross-generic action-adventure films have come to offer escapism in place of disaster and spectacle shot through with state-of-the-art special effects. With popularity breeding further popularity, this new over-arching trend is best typified by the cause-and-effect of successful films leading to sequels, trilogies and series. Hence, for example, the ongoing *Star Wars* saga, the *Superman* films (1978–87) the *Alien* series (1979–97), the *Indiana Jones* trilogy (1981–93), the *Rambo* films (1982–88), the *Terminator* films (1984–91), the *Lethal Weapon* series (1987–98), the *Die Hard* trilogy (1988–95) and the *Batman* series (1989–97). These films and their kin have consistently featured in the top ten box-office entries for their respective years (see Kramer 1999; Neale 2000). From seemingly super humans to super-cops and superheroes, collectively such films do indeed appear to have developed as the perfect 'antidotes to disaster' (Ryan & Kellner 1988: 57).

What is particularly interesting, however, are the ways in which action and science fiction blockbusters have still gone on to use disaster as that threat which must be overcome or, better still, prevented. They allow for both continuity and development, as much reformulation as utter relief. As Michael Ryan and Douglas Kellner point out, the same 'fears and desires' articulated in disaster movies of the early to mid-1970s would duly go on to be addressed and 'answered' in blockbusting films like *Star Wars*, *Close Encounters of the Third Kind* (1977) and *Raiders of the Lost Ark* (1981). Such films represent a transformation rather than a clean break, their principal ideological move being to turn 'anxiety' into 'affirmation' (Ryan & Kellner 1988: 57). What is most significant in characteristic ideological accounts of Hollywood cinema of the 1970s and 1980s are the ways in which disaster movies take on both transitional and retrospective importance. So while, on one level, Ryan and Kellner present disaster movies as a regressive and reactionary step back for the New Hollywood, in contrast to the blockbusting adventure films that were to follow in their wake, the inadvertent invitation is to look back on disaster movies as relatively radical and complex. This becomes even more apparent in Robin Wood's account, wherein *The Poseidon Adventure*, *The Towering Inferno* and *Earthquake* are seen as the very epitome of 'disintegrative' cinema. This is an embedded, thematic distinction that becomes even more manifest in contrast to the subsequent 'escapist' cinema initiated by the likes of *Rocky* (1976), *Star Wars* (1977) and *Star Trek* (1979) (Wood 1986: 28). Where disaster movies of the early to mid-1970s were both welcomed and dismissed as escapist entertainment, they can now be looked back on as offering bare survival.

Rather than reflecting back on the 1970s, the following chapter looks at the ways in which familiar elements of the 1970s disaster cycle were to feature in a new wave of action movies from the late 1980s onwards. Providing for both ongoing continuity and pertinent developments, these action movies were to provide disaster with a renewed hybrid existence until the re-emergence of disaster movies – in both concentrated and recycled form – in the late 1990s. The *Die Hard* films, in particular, explicitly recycle elements of the 1970s disaster cycle. By focusing on the *Towering Inferno* dynamics of *Die Hard* (1988), the *Airport* action of *Die Hard 2* (1990), and other films from the '*Die Hard*' genre, we will examine some of the principal comparisons and contrasts between disaster movies and recent action movies, looking at both formal and contextual differences and developments.

Action and Disaster

Like disaster movies – or, indeed, any genre – action movies allow for consideration of formal, industrial and ideological properties. Beginning with the formal differences inherent in the very terms 'action' and 'disaster', for their part, disaster movies are innately passive and survivalist (in the sense that when their central disasters occur the characters have no choice but to try and make their way up, down or out into safety). Where action sequences occur in disaster movies it usually applies to taking control of the situation. Attempts at rescue are the most common activities, but more notable action sequences from the 1970s disaster cycle would include Richard Roundtree's Evel Knievel-style attempt to save a boy caught in the middle of electric cables while water rushes down a reservoir channel in *Earthquake*, or the gunfights that punctuate *Beyond the Poseidon Adventure* (1979). Conversely, action movies are innately active and escapist. Where disaster is an ever-present threat it invariably leads to a race against time or provides a veritable challenge, and where disasters actually occur in action movies they allow for rescue and/or revenge.

Superman (1978) is particularly symptomatic of the ways in which disaster would go on to be reformulated and confronted in the often combined action and science fiction blockbusters that were to follow on from disaster movies in the late 1970s. Beginning with the destruction of Superman's home planet – and this points to the film's science fiction origins – the subsequent adventures on Earth provide for all manner of disaster-and-rescue sequences. These range from a helicopter crashing down the side of a building and a plane hit by lightning to the film's disaster-movie climax, wherein the evil Lex Luthor's missile hits the San Andreas Fault and causes a massive earthquake, itself leading to a derailed passenger train and a bus hanging from the side of a collapsing bridge. Continuity is maintained by the fact that Superman is actually too late to save Lois Lane from getting crushed to death. The solution, however, is a wonderful piece of superhero trickery, with Superman going on to reverse the main effects of the disaster by pulling the Earth back in time by a few minutes. Where was Superman when we needed him in the early 1970s?

The dominant ideological approach to the respective action and disaster movie genres has been to read them in terms of 'reflection' and/or 'compensation'. The 'and/or' is important in this respect because it allows for certain developments, transitions and overlap. Thus, disaster movies of the early 1970s were fully in keeping with the doubt and distrust engendered by Vietnam and Watergate; the films clearly wallowing in disaster yet offering alternatives in the form of strong leadership. From 1974–79, while disaster movies can be seen as reflective of the further uncertain mood following the interim presidency of Gerald Ford, the withdrawal from Vietnam and the ineffectual presidency of Jimmy Carter, similarly for every rudderless plane there was also a brave pilot ready to take control. For its part, a key film like *Star Wars* can be seen as reflective to a certain extent (its 'New Hope' engendered by the new start which Carter's election victory seemed to promise) but, principally, it re-enacts Vietnam in space, the rebels win and the corrupt politicians of the evil Empire are duly despatched.

While *Rocky*, *Star Wars*, *Superman* and the like can be seen as compensating for the ongoing fatigue of the late 1970s, in the 1980s political developments were such that consequent films such as *Raiders of the Lost Ark* and the *Rambo* films took on a thoroughly reflective meaning. Solving the Iranian hostage crisis in an instant, bringing economic prosperity to the country and reinstating America's status as world superpower, Ronald Reagan's presidency affected the move from distrust to optimism. Either avoiding the subject of disaster completely or confronting – rather than succumbing to – the merest threat, science fiction, fantasy, action and adventure films went on to characterise, as much as they were characterised by, the 1980s; the excitement of these films essentially drawing audiences into the prevailing mood of relief and reinvigorated strength (see Wood 1986; Ryan and Kellner 1988; Jeffords 1994).

Partly initiated by the fact that Lucas-Spielberg productions such as *Star Wars* and *Raiders of the Lost Ark* variously make nostalgic use of adventure and science fiction serials, swashbucklers, westerns and war films, while the return to prior modes of derring-do and heroic action is, on one level, thoroughly in keeping with what Susan Jeffords terms 'the Reagan imaginary' (1994: 62), they have also had the effect of drawing attention to a whole history of action and adventure films. Hence the cross-generic, and even retroactive, term 'action-adventure', a formulation which takes us from Robin Hood to Rambo and Tarzan to The Terminator. Where generic and ideological readings prevail, similarly the recent turn afforded by the term 'action/spectacle cinema' has been to bring attention (back) round to the commercial aesthetics of action and spectacle both past and present (see Arroyo 2000). One of the most useful accounts of recent action movies in this respect, particularly in their resurrection and reformulation of disaster, is screenwriter Larry Gross's 'Big and Loud' (1995). However much such films may be dismissed as popcorn fodder, Gross defends 'the Big Loud Action Movie' (as he lovingly calls it) on the grounds that action has always been part of the cinema of spectacle, from *The Birth of a Nation* in 1915 to *Batman Forever* and *Die Hard with a Vengeance* in 1995. More specifically, however, Gross goes on to make the case for Irwin Allen as 'The Master Without Honour', a producer whose films can well be said to have influenced action directors of the 1980s and 1990s.

While the 'majority of critical ink' has been spent on his avant-garde contemporaries, what is often ignored in many academic treatments of Hollywood cinema of the early 1970s is that Allen was the king of popular cinema, making 'shitloads of money' with *The Poseidon Adventure* and *The Towering Inferno*. Even though such films were low on the 'cruelly interpersonal action-adventure violence' that we have become accustomed to in the 1980s and 1990s, 'nonetheless gut-churning jeopardy fuelled every minute of their narrative structure'. Disaster movies of the 1970s were lean, mean, killing machines which relied upon man battling the elements rather than men fighting each other, but their hardy scenarios have become a common feature of recent action cinema. Gross comments that:

> No dramatic experience other than imminent death was ever allowed on-screen, and they were films utterly involved in the romance of spectacular technology. They were films as engineering problems, something that men like James Cameron and John McTiernan have subsequently shown enormous interest in. The first two *Alien* movies and the first two *Die Hard* movies are in one important sense simply Irwin Allen movies, though much better directed and much more intricately produced. An implacable killing force/situation is unleashed in an isolated space and on a small group of people, resulting in one spectacular disaster/death after another, until the force/situation is either subdued or escaped. (1995: 8)

The *Die Hard* films, in particular, explicitly invite comparisons with 1970s disaster movies.

Die Hard

Die Hard opens with a shot that would have been welcome in Chapter 1: a plane landing safely in the clear light of day. While it might be quite common for a film to open with the arrival of its central character, what follows is a businessman talking to the nervous passenger next to him in a manner not too far removed from disaster movie prescience: 'You don't like flying, do you? ... You wanna know the secret to surviving air travel? After you get where you're going take off your shoes and your socks, and then walk around on the rug barefoot and make fists with your toes ... Trust me, I've been doing it for nine years'. When the nervous passenger, John McClane (Bruce Willis), gets up and the businessman sees his gun holster, McClane replies, 'It's okay, I'm a cop. Trust me, I've been doing this for eleven years'. This dialogue between the experienced passenger and the experienced cop perfectly establishes the dialogue between the respective disaster and action movie genres, the one superstitious and the other

completely self-reliant but with each confident in their respective territo-
ries. Even more significant, perhaps, is that when McClane does get to
where he is going, whilst the passenger's solution appears to work, a lot
of pain ensues when McClane has to run around barefoot in a building full
of shattered glass. The advice thus applies much more to *Airport* films and
not high-rise *Towering Inferno* situations.

If McClane is already in some sense a fish out of water, having travelled
from New York to Los Angeles, the Nakatomi Plaza represents a whole different world entirely. This is where his wife Holly (Bonnie Bedelia) works,
and it becomes clear that she and McClane have become temporarily separated because of their jobs, with him staying committed to being a New
York cop and her having chosen a high-flying career at the brand new West
Coast base of the Japanese Nakatomi Corporation. The differences in life-
style are quickly established in McClane's discomfort with the limousine
that has been sent to pick him up and his initial unease with the ultra-
modern Nakatomi Tower itself. With their daughter waiting for both of them
to come home for Christmas, what the opening scenes also establish, of
course, is the personal rift that will go on to be healed by the perilous action
of the film. In contrast to the group dynamics of 1970s disaster movies,
more recent action movies tend to focus on singular heroes with specific
family backgrounds, the main problematic being that the (male) hero's marriage or relationship has already been put under stress by the very nature
of his dangerous peace-keeping job. It naturally follows that, particularly
where the wife or girlfriend is caught up in the crime/siege scenario, the
hero's successful completion of the calamitous task at hand is responsible
for actively bringing them back together, the duress of the situation having
imbued their relationship with renewed perspective.

Although prefigured to a certain extent in the family problems of 1970s
disaster movies, there are sound contextual reasons for this particular relationship aspect of recent action movies, not least the politically correct
turn embodied in the figure of the 'New Man'. There are also sound demo-
graphic factors, however, and in his account of producer Joel Silver, Rick
Altman finds other reasons for the cross-generic, cross-gender and, to a
lesser extent, perhaps, interracial mix of the *Die Hard* films (the race aspect

becoming much more apparent in the third film, *Die Hard with a Vengeance*). Partly practised in the 'buddy pairing' action comedy, *48 Hrs* (1982), Silver's *Lethal Weapon* (1987) and *Die Hard* perfected the formula by combining 'tongue-in-cheek dialogue with thrills and action heightened by time pressure' (Altman 1999: 46). Where action movies have an assumed masculine appeal, Silver's rationale for the more comedy-related, wisecracking aspect of *Die Hard* is that it broadened the appeal of an ostensibly male genre to women: 'The action-genre audience roughly tops out at $60 million. The shitty ones do 40, 45. But if women come, it'll go more than that. *Die Hard* did $82 million because it attracted women' (quoted in Altman 1999: 46–7).

What such a formal, commercial explanation ignores is the fact that gender and, again to a lesser extent, race, also work in the content of *Die Hard*. Hence, as signalled above, McClane's relationship with Holly, placing the emphasis more on romance than comedy. Although less apparent than the interracial pairing of Riggs (Mel Gibson) and Murtaugh (Danny Glover) established in *Lethal Weapon*, in *Die Hard* McClane's main confidante is the happily married black cop, Al (Reginald VelJohnson). This partly mirrors the relationship between lone cop, Riggs, and family man, Murtaugh, but in similar climactic scenes where Riggs and Murtaugh pull their guns simultaneously in shooting the main villain, in *Die Hard* it is left to the previously passive Al to pull the gun on a raging terrorist while McClane is embracing Holly (or, Al finds action while McClane is diverted expressing emotion). Marital relationships and race relations are thus often combined in the buddy pairings of recent action movies.

A principal thread that has been drawn through spectacle, gender, and race in recent action movies is the specific issue of masculinity. Jeffords introduces links between spectacle and masculinity in the following way:

> US masculinity in Hollywood films of the 1980s was largely transcribed through spectacle and bodies, with the male body itself becoming often the most fulfilling form of spectacle. Throughout this period, the male body – principally the white male body – became increasingly a vehicle of display – of musculature, of beauty, of

FIGURE 4 *Die Hard: Beyond the Towering Inferno*

physical feats, and of a gritty toughness. External spectacle – weaponry, explosions, infernos, crashes, high-speed chases, ostentatious luxuries – offered companion evidence of both the sufficiency and volatility of this display. (1993: 243)

In specific terms, Jeffords follows the argument that, moving away from the blatant display of the Reaganite body and partly engendered by the softer rhetoric of the Bush years, since the early 1990s masculinity has come to express itself through more internal and emotional routes. Although Jeffords sees McClane as belonging to the former mode, the transitional nature of the *Die Hard* films is such that he develops through to the latter: 'What Hollywood culture is offering, in place of the bold spectacle of male muscularity and/as violence, is a self-effacing man, one who now, instead of learning to fight, learns to love' (p. 245).

What is most striking in analyses of the hybrid nature of the *Die Hard* films (from Altman's generic account to studies of masculinity) is that disaster movies are rarely mentioned, when, actually, the hyperbolic spectacle is very much due to their use of disaster scenarios – moving the action away from simple car chases, for example, into even more ingenious moments of waste and display. Where disaster movies are mentioned it is invariably to criticise the lack of originality in recent action/disaster films. Andrew Britton's argument that *The Towering Inferno* signalled the beginning of the end for the New Hollywood – the move towards 'mindless spectacle' – is particularly relevant in this respect; in which case *Die Hard* does indeed 'add insult to injury' (Tasker 1993b: 61). It seems that even where the *Die Hard* films do recycle elements of disaster movies in a playful, knowing manner – with McClane in effect deflecting danger through wisecracks – masculinity is expressed and tested even further through the resulting combination of action and disaster.

Similarly, class is an issue borrowed from disaster movies which has only been analysed in relation to action movie dynamics. As Yvonne Tasker argues, 'In the action cinema struggles over position and authority, military rank for example, serve metaphorically as a space for problematics of class' (1993: 238–9). Although action movies can be said to be seizing upon an open convenience in this respect, comparisons can be drawn with the ways in which disaster movies also use professional status (the jobs of the characters) and assumed authority (how characters fare in the attempts at survival) as shorthand expressions of class. This becomes most

apparent when Tasker states that McClane is always 'out of place', referring to both literal dis-locations and his symbolic class position. Hence, as
already mentioned, McClane is a New York cop who has travelled to Los
Angeles and, furthermore, he goes on to fight a group of European terrorists who take control of the Japanese Nakatomi Tower. Like so many characters in 1970s disaster movies, McClane finds himself more or less isolated,
and in unfamiliar surroundings. Similarly, hounded by bureaucratic police
officials on the one side and fighting criminals on the other, McClane goes
on to find himself in the middle of a crossfire of rules and transgressions:

> By and large the hero of the recent action cinema is not an emissary
> of the State ... The hero may be a policeman or a soldier but he more
> often than not acts unofficially, against the rules and often in a reac-
> tive way, responding to attacks rather than initiating them ... In the
> *Die Hard* films McClane, like so many action heroes, opposes him-
> self to authorities that are both bureaucratic and duplicitous. (1993:
> 241)

Again, whilst common to almost all American film heroes (from James
Cagney gangster movies via Clint Eastwood's Dirty Harry, through to the
Rambo films, for example) this anti-bureaucratic stance is familiar to certain class-based frictions dramatised in the 1970s disaster cycle. What such
accounts offer, then, is a way in to understanding how the *Die Hard* films
make similar use of pre-existing disaster movie conventions and issues,
albeit with hybrid inflection and located in a different context, both of
which allow for equally pertinent contrasts.

Terrorist solutions?

As we have seen, disaster movies of the 1970s did not so much have an
enemy as a cause. While the disasters may well have resulted out of the
irresponsible deeds of mad bombers and corrupt capitalists, the raging elements then took over as judge, jury and executioner. The main difference
with action movies is that the action usually results out of a direct battle

between hero and villain. But *Die Hard* also inserts a thoroughgoing disaster scenario between the hero and main villain, ensuring as much intermediate destruction as possible before the final, face-to-face confrontation. If the Nakatomi Tower can be considered the disaster arena in this respect, the active cause of what might loosely be termed disaster is the terrorist group. They themselves are established as an implacable enemy, a Teutonic force going about their business with military precision and technological know-how, in effect using the technological advances of the building to their advantage. Following the basic narrative shift of celebration interrupted by disaster evidenced in *The Poseidon Adventure* and *The Towering Inferno*, after securing the building the terrorists make their way up to the Christmas Party and the terror begins.

The move from 'disaster' to 'terrorism' is not merely the chronological result of 1970s disaster movies giving way to 1980s action movies. The transition, or reformulation, can be partly negotiated by the fact that the origins of *Die Hard* actually lie in the early 1970s. When Roderick Thorp's novel, *The Detective*, was filmed in 1968, Thorp worked on the script for a sequel. Having read a disaster-themed novel called *The Glass Inferno*, Thorp pitched an idea for a sequel in which the detective, Joe Leland, becomes trapped in a Claxxon Oil Corporation skyscraper when a group of German terrorists seize control; the focus of the story provided by the fact that Leland's daughter and grandchildren are also trapped in the building. The project was brought to a halt when Frank Sinatra turned down the deal, but both *The Glass Inferno* and Thorp's subsequent novel, *Nothing Lasts Forever*, would resurface in other film projects. *The Glass Inferno* and a similar novel, *The Tower*, became the combined sources for *The Towering Inferno*. *Nothing Lasts Forever* resurfaced fifteen years later when Joel Silver, looking for ideas for his next action movie, found Thorp's novel in the Fox archives. The combined cop thriller, disaster and terrorism elements thus become intertwined, international terrorism being as much an issue in the 1970s as the 1980s, the cop genre having been given new life by *Bullitt* (1968), *The Detective* (1968), *The French Connection* (1971), and *Dirty Harry* (1971), and disaster movies, of course, being a popular genre when Thorp first put pen to paper. While the middle-aged, middle-class

'Joe' would become the young, working-class 'John', the terrorist group were to remain an identifiably European threat and the action and disaster came to be duly exaggerated.

In keeping with its ostensible cop thriller origins, the main continuity is provided by the fact that in *Die Hard* the terrorists are little more than hi-tech criminals. As it turns out, the terrorist group's stated mission to strike at the heart of corporate greed in order to force the release of other terror-ist freedom fighters is merely a ruse. It's a smokescreen for their real mis-sion, which is to get away with $640 million worth of barrow bonds. If we focus in on the leader, Hans Gruber (Alan Rickman), we might be able to specify what the film is trying to say in this respect. With an English actor playing a ruthless German character, he is a cross between a gentleman villain and an anachronistic Nazi. Without wishing to offend any particular terrorist group, and in any case using terrorism as a general issue, the film thus presents us with a splinter group straight out of a World War Two film in contemporary guise. Of all their modern accruements, Hans's filofax is a particularly telling sign of the times. As the gun-toting soldiers circle the hostages, Hans addresses the crowd with reference to notes scribbled in his filofax. If Holly's nuisance co-worker, Ellis, represents a weak, double-trading yuppie (he later attempts to make a deal with Hans and gives away McClane's identity), Hans, with his smart suit, filofax and the attempt to steal £640 million, could be said to be more like an embezzling boss.

This fine line between terrorism and robbery has already been broached in relation to *Airport*'s mad bomber and *Airport '77*'s professional art thieves, for example. The latter could be considered the nearest equiva-lent but the point is that the hijackers in *Airport '77* were killed as soon as they accidentally crashed the plane into an oilrig. It takes a lot longer to dispense with Hans's group. Whereas in disaster movies the central disas-ter picks off as many innocent as irresponsible characters, the very action of action movies is dependent upon the hero killing the villains ahead of them wreaking any more havoc and claiming more victims. In this move from passive to active, the other main difference is that whereas the inno-cent victims in disaster movies can only find strength in group action and follow their leader, in action movies the individual hero takes over against the odds. With its mixture of action and disaster, *Die Hard* does blur some of the distinctions – a few hostages and members of the rescue services are killed, and McClane does rely on some outside help – but the film clearly stamps its hero's pedigree in terms of popular heroes of the past. As Hans questions McClane via a walkie-talkie: 'Just another American who saw too many movies as a child? Another orphan of a bankrupt culture who thinks he's John Wayne, Rambo, Marshall Dillon?'. If Hans and his group are straight out of a war film (and the hostages straight out of a disaster movie), McClane's preferred archetype is Roy Rogers. He is, of course, a channel-hopping mix of cop, Rambo, and cowboy, but he is the epitome of the self-reliant, self-effacing modern hero, squaring up to the technological terrorists with ingenuity and true grit. In his 1989 critique of the film, 'The White Man's Mythic Invincibility', Maurice Yacowar sees *Die Hard* as essentially reactionary, nothing less than sexist, racist and xenophobic. In referring to American heroes of the pop-cultural past, the film merely makes the conflict between old-fashioned 'American individualism' and modern-day 'corporate Japan/Europe' even more ingrained. Yvonne Tasker's response is that Yacowar himself should be less bureaucratic in his reading. In making essentially playful use of previous film genres, *Die Hard* both pre-empts certain criticisms and opens out a range of possible opinions (Tasker 1993b: 63–4). European audiences are more likely to agree with Hans's acid comments.

Allied to the film's playful valorisation of heroic individualism, the other main contrast to 1970s disaster movies is that the otherwise helpful groups in *Die Hard* are presented as bumbling and incompetent. In the first instance, it is not so much the LAPD and their siege squad who are at fault as the by-the-book orders barked at them by their bureaucratic boss, leading them into certain doom. From his own perspective as an intermediate lieutenant, McClane can only communicate with fellow cop, Al, and rage against a Deputy Chief of Police overly concerned about public relations and preventing property damage. As Hans states, such regulation police work is actually 'necessary' for his plan to work, creating as much diversion as possible so that his mercenaries can get on with the real job of cracking the safe. Similarly, when the bullish FBI officers arrive, they predictably cut electricity supplies to the plaza and unsuspectingly open the safe. As Al says to McClane: 'They've got the Universal Terrorist Playbook and they're running it step by step'. The other nuisance system in the film is the media, with the opportunist news reporter, Thornberg (William Atherton), desperate enough for ratings and fame to invade Holly's house, question her children and in the process signal to Hans that one of the hostages is, in fact, McClane's wife.

With specific regard to the action of the film, although the Nakatomi Tower is not as tall as the skyscraper in *The Towering Inferno*, note the way in which both buildings are cut down to the essentials of action and disaster. When the fire takes hold in *The Towering Inferno*, the lobby is used as an emergency centre, the fire fighters bravely work their way up and down the middle floors, and most of the main characters are trapped on the sixty-ninth floor. In *Die Hard*, the terrorists use the lobby as their operations centre, McClane gets involved in a range of problems up and down the middle floors, and the hostages are held firm on the thirtieth floor. McClane does take refuge in the incomplete floors leading up to the roof, but after setting off the fire alarm, in order to alert the police to the situation, he also draws the terrorists' attention. After the first shootout he is left to evade capture by crawling up, down and along elevator and ventilation shafts. Like Paul Newman trying to get to the promenade room via the mangled staircase in *The Towering Inferno*, or Steve McQueen trying the same up the lift shaft, McClane also has to survive the building itself and the situation is further compounded by the fact that gunfire follows him wherever he goes.

If gunfire can be considered the action movie equivalent of fire in this respect, this is not to forget that recent action movies also feature major explosions. The two biggest bangs in *Die Hard* provide for further correspondences with *The Towering Inferno*. The first explosion is actually the result of McClane turning the terrorists' main weapon against them. After they ambush the siege squad, McClane throws one of the terrorist's detonators down the lift shaft, bringing devastation to the lower floors. There might be an equivalent here in the way that Newman and McQueen have to blow the water tanks at the end of *The Towering Inferno*, a dangerous explosion that will hopefully result in the fire, the main cause of disaster, being extinguished. This is a very loose comparison but a nearer equivalent would be the attempted helicopter rescues near the end of each film. In *The Towering Inferno* the first plan to evacuate the survivors results in the helicopter crashing into the roof, in effect cancelling that area out as an escape route. In *Die Hard* a group of hostages is led to the top of the building but McClane has to head them off because he knows that the terrorists are going to blow the roof. He does turn the hostages back but not in time to warn the FBI helicopters, which in any case open fire on McClane, thinking that he is a terrorist. The roof explodes, the helicopter burns, and McClane is left grabbing onto a fire hose and plummeting down the side of the building. Holding onto the fire hose and blasting the windows open with his gun, McClane is saved by a disaster movie prop and follows through with action movie firepower.

Die Hard 2

Weighing up the relative developments, *Die Hard* provides for more action than *The Towering Inferno* but less disaster. For its part, however, *Die Hard 2* includes more action than all of the *Airport* films put together, and features a central plane crash which is much more devastating than mere 'planes in peril' heading for a relatively safe landing. This is a sequel almost entirely predicated on the fact that it is a sequel. On one level this is indicated in the film's promotional tagline, 'Die Harder', promising more action than its predecessor. And on the level of disaster, why not? *Airport* developed into a series and the 1970s disaster cycle was itself predicated on the fact that disaster, and bigger disasters at every turn, can happen at any moment. As the tagline to *Die Hard 2* makes this serial link with disaster very apparent: 'They Say Lightning Never Strikes Twice ... They Were Wrong'. Combining action and disaster, however, it must be said that this is a particularly brutal crossover, its central disaster sequence demonstrating that it is not only the terrorists who die harder but a planeload of passengers who die harder than anything previously committed to film.

Sequels invariably work through repetition and exaggeration. In terms of its story, *Die Hard 2* is little more than *Die Hard* in a different setting. It is Christmas again and the main difference is that, this time, Holly has come to visit McClane. The film thus saves itself more time by starting and staying in Washington's Dulles Airport, and in a sense follows on from where the opening scene of *Die Hard* left off – with McClane ultimately forced to overcome his fear of flying in very extreme circumstances. McClane's car is towed away, the airport is snowed in and the point about Holly's plane is that it does not get to land until the end of the film. The terrorist plot this time revolves around a military group waiting for the arrival of a South American cocaine smuggler they deem a 'political prisoner', taking over the airport's communication systems and free to hold or crash the incoming passenger jets as they please. With regard to the other characters in *Die Hard 2*, mutual respect is instant in the case of the chief engineer and janitor, earned in the case of the air traffic control manager and won in the case of the initially bureaucratic airport police. Thornberg returns, this time very literally as the nuisance passenger, and the female reporter on the ground turns out to be quite useful. The only twist is that the anti-terrorist squad turns out to be in league with the terrorists and so McClane has to fight turncoats as much as criminals. The greater the betrayal and the larger the disaster, the more help is needed.

Where the story represents so much repetition – albeit with a few more characters added to the mix – the exaggeration becomes most apparent in the combined action and disaster of *Die Hard 2*. With particular regard to its central disaster sequence, the radical sight of watching a plane actually crash and burn is enough to disturb (or, indeed, satisfy) fans of both action and disaster movies. For all of their implied promises of death and destruction, action and disaster movies are highly moral affairs, the bodycounts relating to how many criminals and cowards there are. Combining the two, what was wholly unthinkable in the *Airport* films is brought about by what might be considered equally unthinkable with regard to action movies – namely that the hero does not get to save the plane in time. Rather than reassuring us with its combined action and disaster movie conventions, therefore, *Die Hard 2* undercuts reinforced expectations. McClane may well get his own back later, but for now there is even a further edge in the implication that he is partly responsible for the disaster. This is broached in a casual fashion but it could be, in fact, that McClane himself is a jinx, or at least a man with too much of a nose for trouble. As Al says to him after receiving the faxed fingerprints of McClane's first victim: 'Ouch, when you get those feelings insurance companies tend to go bankrupt'. The film does at least joke about its recurring character in this respect. As McClane says when he makes his way towards the annex: 'Oh man, I can't fuckin' believe this, another basement, another elevator. How can the same shit happen to the same guy twice?'. But there are no self-conscious wisecracks when the film's hero does not get to the annex in time to save the siege squad and the back-up antenna is blown up.

The airport is now thoroughly cut off from the outside world and the terrorists have gained complete control of communications. Worse follows when McClane's actions and subsequent haranguing lead the terrorist leader, Colonel Stewart (William Sadler), to demonstrate his power:

Stewart: This country's got to learn that it can't keep cutting the legs off men like General Lorenzo. Men who have the guts to stand up against Communist aggression.
McClane: And lesson one starts with killing policemen? What's lesson two, the neutron bomb?
Stewart: No, I think we can find something in-between ...

One hour into the film, the terrorists take control of the central landing system and calibrate it to sea level. They tell Windsor Flight 114 to make its landing, feeding false information and benefiting from the fact that the snowstorm blurs their visual approach to the runway. The passengers and crew are oblivious to what is going on in the airport, and the stewardess says to a nice little old lady: 'We're just like British Rail, love, we may be late but we get you there'. McClane gets to the runway and tries to signal with a flare but the plane hits the runway and explodes into a violent inferno. Stewart's 'object lesson' is complete, and all that remains is a burning wreck, the emergency services left mopping up the damage and McClane holding the remains of a burnt-out doll. Thirteen planes are left circling the airport and Holly's plane only has a limited amount of fuel left. This is a lethal sequence of events. The crash sequence may well add fiery urgency to McClane's ultimate victory but *Die Hard 2* is most definitely the film least likely to appear as an in-flight movie.

Action and destruction

If the general ideological gloss of the *Die Hard* films is that they offer wish-fulfilment solutions to imaginary terrorist incidents, there is something exciting about *Die Hard* that fails in *Die Hard 2*. Although more realistic in certain respects (being based on a common terrorist target and stretch-ing the dilemma to breaking point), perhaps it is far too sensitive to ask how we might regard *Die Hard 2* in light of the 1988 Lockerbie bombing, for example. This would be reading far too much into and out of a film whose sole commercial requirements were to top its predecessor in terms of both action and disaster (a strategy which seems to have worked, with *Die Hard 2* going on to gross $117 million at the US box-office). The difference with the third film, *Die Hard with a Vengeance*, is that it actually deviates from the identifiable disaster formula of the previous two, totally outstripping what might be considered the next equivalent in mind, *Earthquake*. There is also an interesting change of character as the divorced, washed up, semi-alcoholic McClane forges a post-*Pulp Fiction* relationship with Samuel L. Jackson's character, Zeus. The change in context, however, is particularly interesting.

In 1993 international terrorism became an acute domestic concern with the bombing of the World Trade Center in New York, resulting in a feeling of vulnerability further compounded by the 'enemy within' Oklahoma City bombing of 1995. The explosions that open *Die Hard with a Vengeance* certainly echo the attack in New York, but the timing was also such that the ending of the film had to be re-shot in light of Oklahoma (with the action transferred from an exploding building to an exploding boat). However deliberate or accidental, the third *Die Hard* found itself in a situation where terrorism was no longer just a comic book threat or a mere international concern.

On a more basic, generic level, it could be said that *Die Hard with a Vengeance* had to deviate from the norm because the successful action-disaster formula of *Die Hard* had already led to a number of other terrorist action movies that quickly mined all of the remaining disaster staples from the 1970s. '*Die Hard*' has almost become a generic label in own right, in this respect, the first in the trilogy's formative achievement being to resurrect disaster and, through it, enhance the action. Hence *Under Siege* (1992), for example, was commonly referred to as '*Die Hard* on a boat' and *Speed* (1994) '*Die Hard* on a bus'. The case for '*Die Hard*' being a new and very specific generic classification is made by Rick Altman (1999), following on from further examples by journalist Mike Tripplet – '*Die Hard* on a plane' (*Passenger 57*), '*Die Hard* on the president's plane' (*Air Force One*) and '*Die Hard* at a Pittsburgh Penguins hockey game' (*Sudden Death*) (quoted in Altman 1999: 47).

Where such examples point to increasing, doubly derivative, standardisation, of all the films that were to follow the '*Die Hard*' formula, *Speed* remains the most efficient and effective. Partly prefigured in the little-known television disaster movie, *Detour to Terror* (1980), *Speed* simplifies and enhances by making the throttle the trigger, the principal situation relating to the fact that a bomb will explode should a bus full of passengers decrease in speed to under 50 miles-per-hour. Where 'bookend' action sequences in a booby-trapped elevator and an out-of-control metro train fail in comparison with the central hour or so on the bus, they suitably establish the mad bomber's motives and duly conclude with face-to-face combat and a romantic clinch. Filmed 'on location' and directed with expertly engineered flare by Jan de Bont (cinematographer on *Die Hard* and subsequent director of *Twister* (1996)), the bus gradually running out of roads provides for the action-packed essence of the disaster situation. With representative passengers providing for the group element, Keanu Reeve's anti-terrorism expert, Sandra Bullock's bumbling civilian (who has to take over when the bus driver is shot) and Dennis Hopper's Vietnam veteran lunatic very much provide the specific, streamlined, action movie narrative drive.

With a moderate budget of $31 million, *Speed* went on to gross $121 million at the US box office. For its part, the $80 million *Die Hard with a Vengeance* went on to make $100 million. What *Speed* demonstrates, most of all, is effective development of focus and isolation. Although beginning promisingly with a taxi race through New York to defuse a bomb, like the episodic city-wide sprawl of *Earthquake*, in fact, *Die Hard with a Vengeance* goes on to lose its way somewhat, the action progressing onto a subsequent metro rail crash, bank robbery, numerous gunfights and car chases, a flooding tunnel, school building and a boat. It is at this point that the '*Die Hard*' genre was clearly beginning to falter, with 1970s precedents having been fully mined and the films thoroughly repeating themselves. So, where we might say that *Under Siege* is like *Juggernaut*, for example, classifying *Under Siege 2: Dark Territory* (1995) as a variation on *The Cassandra Crossing* must be tempered by the fact that the film probably took place on a train because all other forms of transport had already been used up. Similarly, *Speed 2: Cruise Control* (1997) is much more like *Under Siege* than *Juggernaut*. Costing a reported $100 million and grossing only $48 million at the US box office, while the failure of *Speed 2* can be attributed to the absence of Keanu Reeves or the fact that cruise liners are not renowned for their speed, repetition and lack of inspiration must also be considered.

While the inauguration of the '*Die Hard*' classification can be attributed to the convenience that it has offered to film reviewers looking for pithy summaries of certain action movies, there is no doubt that it does point to an identifiable strain of action-disaster films initiated by *Die Hard*. The resulting trend, however, can itself be qualified in a number of ways, not least the fact that action and disaster increasingly featured in other guises throughout the 1990s. So while, on one level, *Die Hard 2* can be said to have led to the *Airport 1975* variants, *Passenger 57* (1992) and *Turbulence* (1997), and similar capabilities and further inflections appear in the militaristic *Executive Decision* (1996) and presidential *Air Force One* (1997), this is not to forget the fact that plane disasters were not solely restricted to action movies in the 1990s. Hence, for example, the plane crashes which kick-start *Alive* (1992), *Accidental Hero* (1992), *Fearless* (1993), *Random Hearts* (1999) and *Forces of Nature* (1999). Similarly, *Die Hard with a Vengeance* was not the first action movie of the 1990s to focus on bombing campaigns in cities. *Blown Away* (1994) did that in Boston, and while New York has become a major focus, through films like *The Peacemaker* (1997) and *The Siege* (1998), it was principally the Oklahoma bombing that can be said to have inspired the chilling *Arlington Road* (1998) and even *The X-Files: Fight the Future* (1998), which threw a similar incident into its hybrid, plague-ridden, science fiction, conspiracy thriller mix.

The first two *Die Hard* films were specifically predicated on recognisable disaster scenarios from the 1970s, but here we reach the point where 'disaster' has become sheer indiscriminate 'destruction'. That action movies are also prone to a declining imagination of disaster is an argument developed by Kim Newman. As he points out, action movies of the 1980s and 1990s featured plenty of impressive explosions, but by the mid- to late 1990s they had lost all of their glowing impact, 'stripped of metaphor, reduced to simple plot functions, rarely even given the dignity of serving as a given film's actual climax' (Newman 1999: 261). At a time when buildings, various forms of transport and selected cities getting blown up, hijacked and held to ransom had become standard action movie procedures, a number of 'natural' and 'science fiction' disaster movies were to bring disaster back round again in an ever more concentrated and hybrid form in the late 1990s.

3   THE SENSE OF AN ENDING

According to 'Disaster Online', 25 disaster movies were released throughout the 1980s, the most productive year being the 1970s rollover year of
1980. Surpassing even the 1970s disaster cycle, 56 disaster movies were
released in the 1990s, with 14 films released in the peak year of 1997. As
we saw in relation to the 1970s disaster cycle, all these films can be said
to address, with varying degrees of success and sophistication, issues pertinent to the times in which they were made. This approach is, however,
complicated somewhat when it comes to the disaster cycle of the 1990s.
Simultaneously recycling 1950s and 1970s precedents, and tapping into
a number of fashionable anxieties surrounding the run-up to the end of
the millennium, it is difficult to read disaster movies of the 1990s without
reference to previous disaster cycles or, conversely, the altogether hyperbolic prospect of imminent doom. Similarly, where the 1970s disaster cycle
lasted the whole course of a decade, what might be claimed as an equivalent, long-running, 1990s disaster cycle can be qualified in two ways. First
of all, the 1990s cycle refers to a wave of films almost exclusively restricted
to the late 1990s. Secondly, where the 1970s disaster cycle has been read
with specific, identifiable, social and political factors in mind, the concen-
tration of disaster movies in the late 1990s has, indeed, principally led to
them being labelled as 'millennial movies', their main rationale, it would
seem, being to face up to nothing less, and little more, than the end of the
world (see, in particular, Newman 1999).

Certainly, the stakes are generally much higher in the 1990s disaster cycle. Ranging in scope from tornadoes and volcanoes to alien invasion and approaching asteroids, the natural disasters in 1990s disaster movies are overwhelming, and the aliens and asteroids invariably bring the world to the brink of total destruction. Whilst providing their often far-fetched causes of disaster with not altogether inexplicable motives, however, reading disaster movies of the late 1990s solely as 'millennial movies' ignores not only industrial imperatives but also further, ideological readings that can be brought bear on them. With regard to commercial considerations, certainly disaster movies can be said to have tapped into, and further energised, the 'pop millennarianism' of the time; the tabloid stories, television documentaries and best-selling books which effectively worked in turning 'anxiety' into 'interest' (see, for example, Drosnin 1997). More directly, however, the time was ripe for bringing disaster movies back round again. With science fiction B-movies having been out of circulation for over thirty years and disaster movies having become action-disaster movies, audiences could now be reminded of what they had been missing for so long, and most of all, perhaps, with primal scenes of mass destruction having been given a spectacular new sheen by recent advances in computer-generated special effects (see Cubitt 1999; Barker 2000).

Above all, the millennial aspect of 1990s disaster movies provides for exaggeration. This impacts not only upon the greater causes of disaster but also the determined responses that are brought to bear on them. Looking at the responses more closely, however, it becomes clear that they are decidedly 1990s responses. Which is to say that the disasters have the effect of bringing existing social and political themes to light, issues independent of pure *zeitgeist* and characteristic of the 1990s as a whole. What might be regarded as millennial problems, therefore, are met with strictly material solutions. 1990s disaster movies characteristically work through issues of class, race and gender, but more than ever before, explicitly representative of national and even international concerns. In this chapter we will begin by looking at some of the defining characteristics of the 1990s disaster cycle, focusing in particular on *Volcano* (1997) and the 'natural' disaster movies of the time. Specific comparisons and contrasts between

Volcano and *Earthquake* will be examined, thereby opening up an understanding of formal and thematic developments between the 1970s and 1990s. We will continue by examining three of the main science fiction disaster movies of the time – *Independence Day* (1996), *Armageddon* (1998) and *Godzilla* (1998) – focusing on their use of disaster narratives and the issues that are brought to light in exceptional, exaggerated circumstances. We will end by looking at the ways in which, by the summer of 1998, the spectacular extremes of science fiction disaster movies had led to standardisation and repetition. Where science fiction disaster movies of the time are wholly in keeping with *fin-de-siècle* fantasy, aliens, asteroids and a mutant Mother Nature descending upon 'the city that never sleeps' in effect brought the late 1990s disaster cycle to an end.

Volcano

Volcano is part of a long line of natural disaster films. Like *Earthquake*, the film combines aspects of Maurice Yacowar's 'Natural Attack' category with 'The City Fails'. In his 'Natural Attack' category, in particular, Yacowar uses flood and volcano films to structure his main argument relating to the elements. *The Last Days of Pompeii* provides the most obvious template with regard to the latter, and following on from *Volcano* (1953) and *Krakatoa – East of Java* (1968), the continuity of natural disasters is maintained through to the 1970s: 'The flood and volcano films, wherever they are set, bear the moral weight of the urban renewal sagas of Pompeii, Sodom and Gomorrah. Mark Robson's *Earthquake* is a variation on this type' (Yacowar 1977: 91–2). This variation is made clear in 'The City Fails', wherein the modern setting of *Earthquake* makes the destruction of the city much more important than the cause of the disaster. The 1997 *Volcano* goes on to complete the range by imagining what would happen if a volcano erupted in Los Angeles. If *The Last Days of Pompeii* was based on something which actually happened, and *Earthquake* revolved around a catastrophic quake destroying a city renowned for quakes, *Volcano* tries to ring as much recognition and novelty out of the situation as possible. The recognition lies in the film's Los Angeles setting. The novelty results out of the situation wherein, partly to make up for the fact that there are no volcanoes in Los Angeles, the film's solution is to have its volcano erupt from underneath the city. This is also part of the film's 'high concept', of course, but it is important to remember that the disaster genre has always been based around familiarity and novelty. As we saw in relation to the 1970s disaster cycle, what began with a hole in a plane wall ended with a meteor heading towards the Earth. For its part, *Earthquake* obviously had to try and go one better than *The Poseidon Adventure*, and hold its own against *The Towering Inferno* and *Airport 1975*, both of which were also in various stages of production throughout 1974. The increasing size of the disasters throughout the 1970s disaster cycle was further matched by combining the elements and changing the locations – see, for example, the air, fire and water action of *The Towering Inferno* or the underwater plane in *Airport '77*.

When it comes to disaster movies of the late 1990s, again, it would be easy to bracket them all off as 'millennial movies', competing for *zeitgeist* attention before time – or, more precisely, the fad – runs out. But even here there are distinctions to be made between a film like *Independence Day*, on one hand, and *Twister* on the other. Both were released in the same year, but while the former imagines the entire world suddenly under threat from alien invasion, the latter focuses on a Midwest town used to tornadoes but not quite ready for the monsters which are about to hit.

Looking at the summer blockbusters of 1996, scriptwriter David Pirie does mention the general cause-and-effect appeal of terrorist thrillers and end-of-the-world science fiction just in time for the end of the millennium. However, his main argument is that although these films might well have tapped into resonant ideas, it is up to particular, commercially successful products to spark an interest in bringing certain cycles back round again. *Independence Day* and *Mission: Impossible* successfully recycled Cold War alien invasion and super spying, while *Twister* 'appears to herald a new genre altogether, the weather movie. (You thought it was a one-off? Well, other current examples seem to be at an advanced stage, starring volcanoes, floods, and so on)' (Pirie 1996: 26–7). Putting it this way, with full-on 'end-of-the-world' movies on one side and 'weather' movies on the other, we are on our way to specifying certain 1990s disaster

FIGURE 5 *Volcano: Bubbling Under and Over*

movie strands in the same sense that the 1970s cycle could be divided along the lines of 'travel' and 'natural' disasters, as well as 'swarm' and 'monster' movies, for example. Somewhere in between *Independence Day* and *Twister*, for example, we also have 'plague' movies. Sparked by recent concerns surrounding AIDS, the Ebola Virus and 'the New Pandemic' (see Ryan 1996), such films have also benefited from the convenient spread offered by the very nature of contamination. Hence, for example, the two major films of the time range from the small town containment of *Outbreak* (1995) to the post-apocalyptic *Twelve Monkeys* (1995).

What is interesting in Pirie's brief account of weather movies is that he is incorrect in thinking them new but does, almost accidentally, come across a new trend by including volcanoes (arguably more geological than meteorological). Seen in such inclusive terms, the advantage of weather movies is that they are born out of increasing concerns surrounding the environment as a whole. The global causes and effects are far from simple in this respect but, ever since the discovery of the hole in the ozone layer in the 1980s, every hot summer and cold winter, volcanic eruption and vicious hurricane have been regarded as symptoms of an increasingly sick planet (see Radford 1990). Hence, even in this strand of ostensible 'weather' movies, the results vary from the local flooding in *Hard Rain* (1997) to the melting of the polar ice caps in *Waterworld* (1995). Seen with this wider environmental context in mind, *Twister* is like *Outbreak* and *Waterworld* like *Twelve Monkeys*. If plague movies look at the ways in which humans are being poisoned (often dramatised via military-funded biochemical experiments gone wrong), the context is such that weather movies can be read with a similar, environmental message in mind – that we are also poisoning the planet.

The problem with the late 1990s, however, is that pertinent concerns such as global warming quickly bled into rather more hysterical millennial concerns about Satan, aliens and asteroids. Hence disaster became an all-round bandwagon: natural disasters here, aliens there, lava bombs and meteor fragments everywhere. The 1970s cycle was much more specific in terms of both causes and responses (and even, possibly, much more limited as a result). Specific to both cycles, however, are the ways in which Hollywood was to mine the respective contexts and formulae for all they were worth, thus ensuring cycles with more or less definite ends. The most specific instances of scrambling for similar ideas in the 1990s were the two volcano films released in 1997 and the two asteroid movies of 1998. An interesting point about *Dante's Peak* and *Volcano* is that, on hearing of the prospective overlap, Universal and Fox did consider pooling their resources in the same way that Fox and Warner had done with *The Towering Inferno*. Instead, *Dante's Peak* stuck to its topographically correct volcano in a remote Northwest location. In his report on the production of *Volcano*, Benjamin Svetkey is right in pointing out that such clashes were inevitable in the wake of *Independence Day* and *Twister*. The competition was such that the studios were forced to out-do each other and the public were given more of what they seemed to want. 'Disaster is in the air,' states Svetkey, and he offers five telling theories as to why; the first two in terms of context and the other three in terms of the typical Hollywood response:

a) The Big M – Writer Jerome Armstrong: "It's the millennium. Historically, people are always curious about the apocalypse at the end of a century. Look at all the renewed interest in all the religious cults. Same thing with disaster movies."

b) The End of History – Producer Shuler-Doner: "We have no more Russians, no more Germans, no more villains. So we turn to Mother Nature."

c) Build a Better Death Trap – Fox chief Laura Ziskin: "The technology has reopened the genre. We now have the capability to execute anything you can imagine."

d) Shut Up and Pass the Popcorn – Writer Billy Ray: "When I'm home flipping the channels and *The Poseidon Adventure* or *The Towering Inferno* comes on, I'm gone for two hours. This type of movie is just a great ride."

e) The Tommy Lee Jones theory: "It has nothing to do with the *zeitgeist*. It has to do with business." (1997: 3–4)

Any and all of these theories perfectly sum up the 1990s disaster cycle.

The coast is toast

Moving on to more specific comparisons and contrasts between *Earth-quake* and *Volcano*, it could be argued, firstly, that these films are the most explicit and sustained natural disaster films of their respective cycles. Where the tidal wave in *The Poseidon Adventure* merely triggers the action, and all manner of avalanches, storms and so on were to provide for altogether standard natural disasters throughout the 1970s disaster cycle, *Earthquake* is punctuated by effective quakes throughout. Similarly, where *Twister* very much set the technical standard with regard to 1990s 'weather' movies, the events take place in a rather more isolated Midwest setting, and partly because the film also focuses so much on its central argumentative, romantic pairing, the representative group element is negligible. Beginning with a range of representative characters, and following through with progressive scenes of metropolitan destruction, *Volcano* positively invites comparisons with *Earthquake* and the 1970s breed of disaster movies. There are a number of key differences, however, which are equally important in distinguishing the 1990s approach from 1970s precedents.

Perhaps the 1970s disaster cycle was so familiar to audiences of the time that *Earthquake* eschewed the usual thrills-and-spills tagline in favour of the much more solid 'An Event...', referring to a suitably epic earthquake fit for an Event Movie. Perhaps we cannot take disaster movies that seriously anymore, hence *Volcano* goes for the much more punning 'The Coast is Toast'. The first thing to say, then, is that *Earthquake* is gritty and determined entertainment. The first line in the film, for example, is Remy's (Ava Gardner) drunken rail at her engineer husband, Stuart Graff (Charlton Heston): 'Goddammit!'. This domestic bile is followed by the first tremor and, frankly, the indications are that, if not necessarily causing the earthquake, there are enough bad vibrations to keep it going. Adding adultery to the mix, Graff tries to find solace in an affair with widowed mother Denise (Genevieve Bujold), the death of whose husband he feels partly responsible for. The film does end with Graff committing himself to saving his wife, but a tenuous grip leads to them being washed down the drain along with their marriage. Other characters of note are Lorne Greene's construction boss (who dies of a heart attack) and Richard Roundtree's stunt biker. One of the most chilling central dramas revolves around Jody (Marjoe Gortner), a fascistic National Guardsman who uses martial law as an excuse to shoot his bullying neighbours, rage against devotees of Hare Krishna and harass the object of his desire, Rosa (Victoria Principal). George Kennedy is solid as ever as the community cop, Slade, and gets to shoot Jody after his attempt to rape Rosa: 'Earthquakes bring out the worst in some guys, that's all'. From domestic strife and adultery to lawlessness and disorder, the social psychology of the film is terrifying. The earthquake both exacerbates and cures, bringing tensions to the surface in order for the shock therapy to begin.

The main hero figure in *Volcano* is Mike Roark (Tommy Lee Jones), divorced father and troubleshooting team leader for the Office of Emergency Management (OEM). With his teenage daughter visiting for the weekend, the characteristic disaster-movie tension between professional duty and domestic commitments is duly brought to the fore when Roark is called in to investigate an underground explosion. But notice the differences between this central relationship and the bitter, crumbling marriage in *Earthquake*. The most curious difference is that Roark's wife remains absent from the film (and due to lack of details, we can only assume that it is his commitment to his job which led to the separation). This removes antagonism from the situation and places the domestic emphasis solely on Roark's relationship with his daughter. The film proceeds with its action so promptly that the problem of Roark committing himself to his job is conveniently solved by the fact that he has his daughter with him when the first major eruption hits.

Both quicker pacing and political correctness distinguish *Volcano* from *Earthquake*, the pacing in effect allowing the film to sketch over certain sensitive or overly problematic details. It is in this combined sense that Roark's relationship with seismologist Dr Amy Barnes (Anne Heche) is barely a conventional 'romantic' relationship at all. In contrast to *Earthquake*, neither adultery nor anguish feature in this professional and ultimately open-ended central pairing. Initial differences of opinion are merely replaced by mutual respect. Principally, however, pacing and political correctness work in removing villains from *Volcano*. The main differences are that, whereas the main construction manager and the fascist guardsman duly die in *Earthquake*, here the film's builder character just leaves and his latest building proves quite useful as a dam, and a racist cop joins with the film's Rodney King figure to shore up the city's defences. With little major personal and social conflict, however, *Volcano* is able to add more speculation to the cause of its disaster. With disruptive psychology removed from the equation, general hubris is joined by a more specific, environmental, message. Given the health-conscious state of Los Angeles there are plenty of cigarette jokes, for example, particularly at the beginning when a shot of the Marlboro Man is followed by a fiery vein developing in the road, and then throughout as the Metro boss decides to take up smoking again. Along with references to traffic pollution, the most specific indication is that the current subway extensions have triggered this long-dormant, underground volcano. The only significant death in the film, therefore, is the Metro boss. The nearest that *Volcano* gets to a principal villain figure, however, melts into the ground slowly enough to redeem himself by saving an unconscious train driver and saying the Lord's Prayer.

There is an interesting formal difference between the two films, in the way that *Earthquake* refers to cinema and *Volcano* refers to television. It is almost imperceptible in the first instance, but there is a definite sense in which *Earthquake* realised that it was part of an established film cycle, and possibly the only new perspective left was to foreground the ways in which audiences of the time were increasingly experiencing disaster through cinema. The Walter Matthau cameo is a strange case in point. Appearing in the credits under his real name, Walter Matuschanskayasky, all that he does throughout the film is drink toasts to film stars. Also, Genevieve Bujold plays a struggling actress in the film. This might be common enough in Los Angeles but there is one scene in particular where she practises her lines with Heston's character: 'I play a bit player. Now the bit you play is a big movie star'. When the earthquake hits, one of the first things to tumble is the mock film set in her house. These moments of self-referentiality are followed through to the main experience of the film.

One of *Earthquake*'s main selling points was the introduction of Sensurround, a short-lived innovation (also used in the war film *Midway* (1976), and the theme-park disaster movie, *Rollercoaster* (1977)) whereby, through a combination of air and low frequency, the rumble of the tremors in the film actively vibrated the cinema (see Holliss 1996). In the same sense that 3D movies of the 1950s looked for all sorts of excuses to stick things into the camera, there is a moment later on when a landslide occurs across the reservoir. One of the workers says, 'Jesus, that's a scary sound'. More specifically, however, when the main quake hits, the first person that we see it happening to is Rosa in a cinema. In a manner not unlike the liquid menace first making its appearance in a small-town cinema in *The Blob*, or the sneeze that first spreads fatal droplets through the crowded cinema auditorium in *Outbreak*, whilst Rosa is watching a Clint Eastwood western, the gunshots are followed by a low rumble. When the Sensurround starts to kick in, the point is that we, the real audience, are experiencing what Rosa is experiencing in that cinema. The LA cinema shakes, the film she is watching melts and the audience around her panics. Rosa comes out of the cinema and then we see what is happening to the rest of the city. The earthquake sequence itself is a composite mix of scenes already evidenced in *San Francisco* and delivered through an attempt at *Battleship Potemkin*-style montage (particularly in a close-up of a woman with glass in her face). The six-minute sequence ends with a strange animated splat of red on the screen when an elevator falls through the floor. *Earthquake* is all about artifice and experience.

One of the messages of *Volcano* is that 'if it's not on television, it hasn't happened' (Tunney 1997: 63). The form of the film is such that the disaster is also covered by a number of television news reports. The narrative convenience of this is best demonstrated when the film takes us through a montage of the city at the beginning, the news reports filling us in on what is happening in LA and allowing the film to introduce its main characters (many of whom have the television on in the background). The technique is such that it also has its satirical moments, but instead of going on to make the critical point that we are all electronic voyeurs, the distance is such that the disaster is 'reduced to a spectator sport with the audience placed in the same, safely sanitised, position as the television viewer' (Tunney 1997: 63). It would, indeed, have been much more dramatic if the film's insulated centres – the television studio and the OEM building – were also hit by lava. The reporting does get more involved later on but, certainly, there is a glossy, omniscient distance to the central newsreaders. When they are ruffled by the first tremors, for example, they come out from under their desks, straighten their ties and promptly move on to the weather. The news helicopters stand in for a National Guard unable to cover all of the emergencies and the coverage becomes a major surveillance source for the OEM. The most chilling moment, however, comes when a man phones a talk-radio station, safely cocooned in his car and neglecting to help when a fire engine and some of its firemen are engulfed by fire.

The context for all of this intertextual media coverage in *Volcano* is the fact that 24-hour news channels have increasingly come to present disaster as live entertainment, the resulting confusion being: are there more disasters than ever before or is there just more television? *Volcano* taps into a number of real-life disasters which hit the Hollywood heartland and were covered live on television throughout the 1990s; principally the LA Riots in 1992 (which, although not a true disaster, were certainly covered like a disaster movie), LA's very own 'Great Quake' of 1994 and, contemporary to the making of the film, the forest fire that went on to burn down several film stars' houses in 1996. Very specifically, the film seeks to make up for the LA Riots. Sparked in response to the release of the police officers who were filmed beating Rodney King, the LA Riots have been seen by many as an eruptive race war (see, for example, Davis 1999).

In contrast to the pervasive social unrest dramatised in *Earthquake*, *Volcano* invites much more specific contextual readings in this respect. Bearing in mind the longstanding feelings and complex issues that came to a head in the LA Riots, however, the film's response is very simplistic. As focused on the black teenager handcuffed to a fire engine by a racist policeman ('I'm about to become the volcano version of Rodney King!'), mass conciliation takes place after he is duly released. The teenager and the policeman, their friends and colleagues, businessmen and looters all join together and plug the lava flow. After the lava has frizzled into the ocean, ash snows down from the sky. All of the survivors are covered in grey flakes and a child says, 'Look at their faces, they all look the same'. More than ever before, perhaps, disaster movies have come to provide simple solutions to complex problems.

Independence Day

Independence Day saves the world through recycling, the principal invitation being to regard it as *The War of the Worlds* in the air and – particularly after the aliens have destroyed Los Angeles – *Earthquake* on the ground (see Newman 1999). This gets to the essence of a film that faces up to the end of the world with sheer nostalgia; finding safety in numbers, almost, by combining science fiction with disaster movie and war film with action-adventure. Given the film's broad sweep of genres, it may prove useful to focus initially on its disaster narrative. The day-by-day progression of the film in effect splits it into three acts:

July 2 Beginning with the arrival of the aliens and ending with the destruction of major cities.

July 3 Beginning with a failed counterattack by the military and ending with the failure of their desperate nuclear solution.

July 4 Beginning with an opportune scientific plan and ending with victory over the aliens.

The problem with reading *Independence Day* as a conventional (that is, 1970s) disaster movie, however, is that the destruction of major cities at the end of Act I – the main disaster – is merely Step One for the aliens, a strategic strike which they plan to follow up with total invasion. Hence the main human characters are seen surviving and then battling their way towards averting the next, final, disaster. In this sense, only the first half of the film could be said to follow the 1970s formula, with a much more proactive solution driving the rest of the narrative. Disaster movies of the 1970s had always tended to absorb the first two components of Nick Roddick's threefold narrative structure, 'the world before the disaster' and 'the disaster itself' (1980: 50) into their first halves. *Independence Day* stretches 'the world after the disaster' through to survival, retaliation and victory, and is much more akin to Susan Sontag's (1965) five main phases of narrative action:

Act I   combining (1) and (2), the arrival of the aliens and the initial demonstration of their power;

Act II combining (3) and (4), the military devising and failing in their counterattack;

Act III following (5) through to the final, successful fight-back.

It is just as well that *Independence Day* falls back on such a reliable science fiction formula because, actually, there is nowhere else to go after the film's rather impressive central disaster sequence. The first 45 minutes of the film are like a tickertape of activity, introducing characters from its four main locations and with the technically minded David Levinson (Jeff Goldblum) working out that the hovering spaceships are counting down to 'checkmate'. Some evacuation plans are carried out but it is too late: 'Time's up'. Los Angeles is incinerated; cars, people and buildings are obliterated in New York; and Air Force One just manages to escape the inferno as the White House and other symbols of democracy are blown to pieces in Washington. Act II opens with the Statue of Liberty lying face down in the river and all devastated cities facing up to the prospect of total invasion. The problem with staging such an impressive and catastrophic spectacle so soon is that it does leave the rest of *Independence Day* in something of a haze. This is understandable as far as the characters and main cities in the film are concerned, but what about the audience? There is some pleasure to be had in the subsequent failed counterattacks, with Captain Steven Hiller (Will Smith) 'anxious to get up there and whup ET's ass' but then seeing his squadron defeated, and President Thomas J. Whitmore (Bill

Pullman) finally looking into the heart of darkness. 'Nuke 'em. Let's nuke the bastards,' he says, only to watch as the stealth bombers fail to make an impact. As far as the final, successful fight-back is concerned, however, Kim Newman is probably right in stating:

> The finale strains hard as overworked effects men try to come up with a climax which tops the holocausts of the first two acts. What the film doesn't manage is to make our inevitable victory over the aliens as convincing as their initial crushing defeat of the Earth. (1999: 125)

There are two responses to the central disaster in this respect. First of all, how did disaster movies of the 1970s maintain narrative momentum after their opening disasters? *Airport* got over this problem by staging its main disaster in the second half of the film – and *Earthquake* compromised by having its main quake early on but with a further lead-up towards aftershocks splitting the Hollywood dam open at the end. But what about *The Poseidon Adventure*, for example? Drown 1,400 people within thirty minutes and what is the viewer left with? The answer here, of course, is survival. *The Poseidon Adventure* does work for a further 90 minutes by putting its relatively interesting survivors in ingenious moments of further peril, the hurdles surmounted in the main but with individual casualties along the way proving as intermittently effective as the mass destruction at the beginning. This works to a certain extent in *Independence Day* – basically the fate of the world in the hands of a strategic group of people – but the second response offered here can be considered a criticism of the negative appeal of disaster. Perhaps it is, indeed, *Independence Day*'s fault: not necessarily for featuring key disaster sequences but leading with them in the film's six-month promotional campaign. The posters may well have led with science fiction (the spaceships gradually approaching Earth as the campaign progressed) but the trailer ended with a bang which, as Michael Rogin argues, elicited a strange reaction, particularly in light of the 1995 Oklahoma City bombing:

Audiences that cheered the White House holocaust might seem to have been mobilised by *ID4* for an assault on the political elite. The graphic destruction of American icons, generating a crowd-pleasing *frisson* more intense than any produced by the familiar science fiction fantasy air battles, did give *ID4* its peculiar appeal. (1998: 39)

In terms of both the narrative and ideology of the film, this particular image of the White House being destroyed was totally misleading. The trailer promised disaster and the film answers with heroism. The trailer proved popular because it showed the President's house (and possibly the President) getting blown up; the film proved popular regardless (and possibly because) of the fact that its young, Clintonesque President rises like a phoenix from the flames. The trailer hints towards the end of the world – or at least American civilisation – and the film has America saving the world. *Independence Day* turns disaster on its head and possibly points the finger at us for being so drawn in by death and destruction in the first place. Survival has become much more important than disaster, 'anxiety' has, indeed, moved on to 'affirmation'.

Saving the world

In terms of its characters, *Independence Day* combines the implied geographical scope of 1950s science fiction B-movies with the microcosmic focus of 1970s disaster movies. Although we knew that the entire world was under threat in 1950s alien invasion movies, the tendency was to focus on a certain city getting destroyed (usually Washington or San Francisco) and with the solutions resulting from a metropolitan alliance of military might and scientific thought. Certain radio and television snapshots did remind us that the whole of America and the rest of the free world, at least, were also under threat but, as focused on these political and intellectual centres, we could be assured that just one (American) victory will lead the way. For all its first sightings, reportage and victory scenes from the rest of the world – the Iraqi desert, the Persian Gulf, London, Moscow, Paris, Sydney, Africa, Egypt and Japan – make no mistake that America also leads the

FIGURE 6 *Independence Day: Earth versus the Flying Saucers*

way in *Independence Day*. The film does have a certain economy, however, through the way in which America is covered by an approximate square route of locations. Cutting a whole country down to four main locations, similarly each of these locations is used to introduce the four main characters: the President in Washington, Levinson in New York, Hiller in Los Angeles, and the washed-up hick, Russell Casse (Randy Quaid), in Nevada. With their respective locations destroyed they all gather in Area 51, a microcosmic group ready to strike back at the cosmic force about to take over the entire world.

One of the main issues which has been related to this particular group is the subject of race. This is interesting as far as the disaster genre is concerned, which, as we have looked at it so far, has tended to focus on issues of class and gender. It is an attempt at least, by no means successful but open to debate. As Amy Taubin introduces the film's view of a thoroughly United States of America:

> *Independence Day* is a feel-good picture about the end of the world, or rather about how the end of the world is averted by good men who put aside their racial and ethnic differences to come together in a common cause. It's the answer to Rodney King's heartbreaking plea in the aftermath of the LA Riots: 'Why can't we all just get along?'. We can, it seems, but only under the threat of an alien invasion. (1996: 6–7)

As Taubin specifies, although *Independence Day* includes visual and verbal references to World War Two, the Cold War, Vietnam and the Gulf War, the aliens are just post-Roswell aliens, tentacled ciphers against which multicultural America (headed by a WASP president) can rail with politically correct impunity. If Whitmore is, indeed, a motivating centre for all of this, the main alliance in the film is that between the African-American Hiller and the Jewish Levinson (with Casse as the 'white-trash alcoholic who's fathered a bunch of ex-Tex-Mex brats' (Taubin 1996: 8)). For all its attempts at political correctness, *Independence Day* has little time for women. The First Lady (Mary McDonnell) becomes a sheer plot device, her death motivating Whitmore into committed action, and the other female characters, the careerist Connie (Margaret Colin) and the reformed stripper Jasmine (Vivica A. Fox), are defined solely in relation to Levinson and Hiller. In introducing a wide variety of representative characters and proceeding at such a quick pace,

Independence Day does trade in stereotypes, but they are stereotypes that come to life in the film's subsequent action. Levinson and Hiller are in many ways held back until given the opportunity to prove themselves. As Levinson's father, Julius (Judd Hirsch), keeps reminding him, having moved away from his family and taken up a mere technician's job, Levinson is a relative under-achiever. Similarly, despite having been promoted to Captain, Hiller's application to join NASA is rejected. As colleague and confidante Jimmy (Harry Connick Jr.) hints, Hiller's decision not to marry his (stripper) girlfriend might have been the deciding factor in this respect. A measure of the way in which *Independence Day* brings Levinson and Hiller together is through their quick-fire banter, a technique wholly in keeping with the ongoing action and a release from the increasing tension. With Levinson providing the technical knowledge and Hiller providing the flying expertise, the aliens are defeated and the end of the world duly diverted (see, also, Rogin 1998).

Armageddon

The opening of *Armageddon* has none other than Charlton Heston narrating the ultimate natural disaster: 'This is the Earth at a time when the dinosaurs roamed a lush and fertile planet. A piece of rock just six miles wide changed all that'. In the same sense that the aliens in *Independence Day* could be said to represent 'environmentally despoiling capitalists who strip-mine and abandon entire planets' (Newman 1999: 124) and are defeated by the eco-friendly Levinson, *Armageddon* works in turning a group of drillers into eco-warriors. We are introduced to Harry Stamper (Bruce Willis) and his team on a Japanese-financed oil rig, with Stamper hitting golf balls at a nearby Greenpeace boat. Part of the response of the film, therefore, is to have these environmentally unfriendly men turned from plundering the remains of dinosaurs and choking the planet to drilling and destroying the approaching asteroid. If environmental readings of the cause of disaster fail because of the external nature of the film's 'global killer', the Bible is also signalled as providing a longstanding motive. Armageddon, of course, is that land in the Book of Revelation to which an already plague-ridden mass is sent to suffer the rest of God's wrath – thunder, lightning and quakes (see Benjamin 1998). With this in mind, perhaps the opening narration, delivered as it is from a suitably God-like perspective by Charlton Heston, ends with a warning rather than a countdown: 'It happened before, it will happen again. It's just a question of when'. The potential effects here on Earth are certainly interpreted in appropriate ways. As NASA's mission controller, Dan Truman (Billy Bob Thornton), explains the need for secrecy: 'There'd be a total breakdown of social services – mass religious hysteria, looting, rioting – basically the worst parts of the Bible'.

Whether environmental in extremis or biblical in precept, the response to the approaching asteroid and its allied fragments is decidedly contemporary and technological. After the beautiful, clinical, God-like perspective of its prelude, *Armageddon* brings us into the present day with a flurry of activity. The shuttle Atlantis is destroyed and the Pentagon suspect a surprise missile attack. Similarly, when the first shower hits New York the sequence is explosive, messy and mortal. The Chrysler Building is cut in half, Grand Central Station is shattered and the World Trade Center is shot to pieces. Bearing in mind the change in context, however, clearly (centralised) Russian missile attack is ruled out. A measure of the post-Cold War compromise of the film, in fact, is that Russia is represented by the dilapidated MIR space station, useful for refuelling but then becoming a hazardous wreck and, similarly, leaving the group with a lunatic cosmonaut who redeems himself at the end. As splinters landing in 'South East Asia' and (most impressively) Paris remind us, the whole world is at stake so unilateral efforts are made, the Hubble telescope used in monitoring the asteroid, for example, and the mission part funded by France and Japan. That it is principally America's job to save the world, however, is clearly indicated when the President goes on to deliver his uplifting crisis speech over a glossy global village composed of the Balkans, Italian churches, the Blue Mosque, Vatican and the Taj Mahal.

The main contrast with *Independence Day* is that *Armageddon* is more of an action movie than a war film. These are all science fiction/disaster hybrids at heart, but further contrasts can be made between films as ostensibly similar as *Armageddon* and *Deep Impact*. Released in the spring of

1998, *Deep Impact* is more of a disaster drama than a disaster movie. One particular comparison made by Philip Strick is that, as directed by former *ER* cinematographer, Mimi Leder, and featuring familiar faces from a range of popular television programmes as well as cameos from her husband and daughter, 'somehow an awesome topic has become an almost cosy family picture' (Strick 1998: 40). Because of the fact that the authorities are given a year's notice, *Deep Impact* is, indeed, a relatively quaint, leisurely stroll of a disaster movie. Its narrative structure is very much in keeping with *When Worlds Collide* (1951) in this respect, the disasters deferred until the very end. By contrast, *Armageddon* follows the *Meteor* route by featuring fragments of destruction throughout. Similarly, *Armageddon* is a very typical Jerry Bruckheimer production. Having perfected his partnership with Don Simpson in *Top Gun* (1986), the Bruckheimer formula has clearly been followed through to more recent, post-Simpson releases, *The Rock* (1996) and *Con Air* (1997), both of which involve tough men taking part in high-powered action. Bruckheimer films are above all efficient and bombastic, their narratives progressing in such a way that the more pressing the dangers, the more deflective wisecracks, male bonding and subsequent nick-of-time heroics are required.

Most of the action in *Armageddon* results from the fact that Stamper's team is a group of workers – the only men skilled enough to carry out the task ahead. After the racial mix of *Independence Day*, we are back to the principal disaster movie subject of class. This sense of rough-and-ready men is clearly established in the film's poster, featuring the group of workers in their spacesuits, and only the inclusion of Liv Tyler, perhaps, altering the blurb: 'For 18 Days The Planet Holds Its Breath. While A Group Of Ordinary People Set Out To Save It'. In contrast to the blue-collar masculine action of *Armageddon*, *Deep Impact* is based on much more abstract values: 'Oceans Rise. Cities Fall. Hope Survives'. 'Hope Survives' is a passive, essentialist solution to a problem that *Armageddon* faces up to with dirty hands and high-powered drills. Repeatedly throughout the film Stamper is referred to as a Red Adair, 'the world's best deep core driller', but fundamentally his leadership principle is tempered with the value of teamwork: 'I'm only the best because I work with the best'. The group is established as generically rough and ready, first rounded up, as they are, speeding, gambling and in stripper joints. Their misdemeanour characteristics are further developed in a few flippant demands to Truman and Colonel Kinsey – deleting some parking tickets, awarding free season passes to Caesar's Palace, letting the group off from paying taxes and possibly providing an answer to the question of who killed Kennedy.

The mutual compromise of the film is that the military have to learn human values (and develop a sense of humour) as much as the drillers need to be redeemed into respectability and responsibility. The immediate link is that between Truman and Stamper. As we find out, Truman missed his opportunity to become an astronaut because of a war injury and joined NASA's engineering program instead. He is thus the decent worker made group leader. Ultimately Truman holds off the military so that Stamper can finish the job, and Stamper reciprocates by sending him his mission patch. Similarly between NASA's abstract scientists and Stamper's hardy workers, each has to put their faith in the other – NASA calculating the mission and providing the shuttles, the drillers providing the manpower and operating the Armadillo. But even the drillers and the military have to meet in the middle. Often presented in slow motion, drum-pulse shots, the first time that the drillers appear in their astronaut suits, Colonel Willy Sharp responds: 'Talk about the Wrong Stuff'. Astronauts are undoubtedly regarded as heroic figures in the film, the jobbing, pioneering reference points being Apollos 1, 11 and 13, but the fact that a special group of airforce astronauts flies the mission makes for further conflict and compromise. This is to say that the squad is a group as the drillers are, and Sharp in the same position as Stamper, but Sharp ultimately answers to military command. When the drilling goes wrong, the military takes over mission control and issues Secondary Protocol, making moves to detonate the nuclear missile from afar. On the shuttle Sharp opens his instructions, allows remote access and prepares to leave. However, Stamper goes on to persuade Sharp with sheer self-reliance: 'Why are you listening to somebody a thousand miles away? We're *here*!'. Thus being here on the mission, carrying out the job, becomes much more important than taking orders from above and beyond: 'Houston, *you* have a problem!'. The final slow-motion group shot of the film, therefore, shows five red suits and two blue, the reds having found the Right Stuff and Sharp saluting Stamper's achievement: 'The bravest man I've ever known'.

Although featuring less death and destruction than *Independence Day*, *Armageddon* tries to end one better by sacrificing its star so that no less than three marriages can take place. Boiling the film down to its essentials, the message is simple: go to work, save the world, get married, populate the species. Where *Die Hard*-style action movies take place in buildings, transport and extend to saving American cities, *Independence Day*, *Deep Impact* and *Armageddon* use their world-saving agendas as an excuse for speaking on behalf of the world (very literally in the case of their respective presidential speeches). If this is their 'global' agenda, their 'national' agendas are played out through relationships, race relations in the case of *Independence Day*, and the nuclear family in the case of *Deep Impact*. In the end, *Armageddon* is as much a 'family values' film as its more soap opera-oriented rival. Where the Holly-McClane relationship is positively central to the narrative drive of the first two *Die Hard* films, and family tensions of prime importance throughout *Deep Impact*, for the most part, male-female relations remain marginal in *Armageddon*. Hence the move towards making them central to the film's conclusion is particularly abrupt. As signalled by the REM song playing on the radio at the beginning of *Independence Day* ('It's the end of the world as we know it, and I feel fine'), the implications are that we are not meant to take this or, indeed, *Armageddon*, too seriously. With 'Boy's Own' heroics and self-effacing pop culture wisecracks taking place in narratives where potential global catastrophe ends up bringing people closer together, above all these films provide an antidote to the end of the world in the form of action, spectacle and sheer escapism.

Godzilla

Whereas *Independence Day* and *Armageddon* variously recycle aspects of 1950s science fiction B-movies, the 1998 version of *Godzilla* is technically a remake of the original 1954 Godzilla film, *Gojira*. While this invites more specific comparisons, differences of both time and place must be taken into account. The leap from Japan in the 1950s to Hollywood in the 1990s can in part be negotiated, geographically, by the fact that *Gojira* was itself influenced by American monster movies. Having already been inspired by repeated viewings of *King Kong* and his visit to Hiroshima in 1946, the success of films like *The Beast from 20,000 Fathoms* (1953) and Disney's *20,000 Leagues Under the Sea* (1954) finally led producer Tomoyuki Tanaka to devising a nuclear monster movie. If his provisional title, *The Big Monster from 20,000 Miles Beneath the Sea*, betrayed the obvious borrowings, Tanaka went on to compromise with a suitably mutant name, Gojira, born out of both 'gorilla' and 'kujira', the Japanese word for a whale.

Essentially, Gojira is a mythical beast given form by context. As the contexts changed, so did the monster. The first change in context was brought about when the film was transferred to America, re-released as *Godzilla, King of the Monsters* in 1956. 'Translating' the film became an excuse for fundamentally changing it, not only in terms of the dialogue, but also in excising certain politically sensitive material, including references to Nagasaki and the more or less explicit fact that the monster was born out of the American H-bomb tests in the Marshall Islands. The other changes in context arose throughout the subsequent decades as a profitable franchise followed. After losing a number of monster fights (including one against King Kong), from 1965 Gojira became a family favourite defending Japan from further topical aberrations like the Smog Monster, Mechagodzilla and Space Godzilla. He did turn to the bad side in 1985 by playing America against Russia – with Japan caught in the middle – but this was just a temporary regression and Gojira died a father to a possible successor and hero to the Japanese people in 1995 (see Hollings 1998; Newman 1999: 87-90).

Given a certain amount of respect for the Godzilla mythology, the $100 million American version partly overcomes the label of travesty by developing elements of continuity through to the new contexts of time and place. A principal technique borrowed from the original *Gojira*, for example, is the gradual appearance of the monster. It begins as a sea beast laying into a Japanese fishing trawler in the Pacific and then swimming to the East Coast of America where it homes in on some fishing boats, tramples New York

Harbour and arrives in Manhattan. Bounding across Panama along the way, the monster leaves a trail of suitably prehistoric footprints and, upon arriving in New York, proceeds to destroy sections of the city with its feet, tail and parts of its head. Throughout, the familiar Godzilla roar accompanies the action and we only get to see the monster in full shot 45 minutes into the film when he is lured out for feeding. Probably the nicest bit of continuity in this respect is that provided by the old Japanese sailor rescued from the trawler. Traumatised and recovering in a hospital in Tahiti, fixing onto the flame from a lighter, he whispers 'Gojira, Gojira'. Godzilla has been passed like a baton from Tokyo to New York, and it is only when the television company gets hold of the hospital footage that 'Gojira' is finally translated: 'A mythological sea-dragon ... our modern terror'.

Finding ourselves in a different time, also, the continuity and development are such that we have moved from the birth of the nuclear age to post-Cold War nuclear testing. The fact that the film is able to begin with the controversial atomic testing in French Polynesia offers a triple convenience – maintaining the nuclear birth of the monster, following it through to the most recent example of Pacific testing, and blaming the French (again, it is not America's fault). The film does, at least, treat the Gallic aspect with a degree of humour, mostly centred on the French secret service agent and 'insurance guy', Philippe Roché (Jean Reno). The usual culture clash jokes apply but even in sending up aspects of American culture – processed coffee, chewing gum, and impersonating Elvis – Roché ends up an American hero of the John Wayne type, and the film does not let us forget that he is there to clear up the 'terrible mess' caused by his country.

If the original Godzilla came to prominence as the physical embodiment of the Nuclear Age and went on to confront other, environmentally unfriendly monsters throughout the subsequent sequels, by introducing its main scientist hero in Chernobyl the 1998 version of *Godzilla* has the advantage of another specific piece of context which combines the nuclear with the environmental – the damaging effects of nuclear contamination. Partly to level out the stock footage and partly to represent the bleached, tropical, nuclear atmosphere, French Polynesia is bathed in yellow, but for its part Chernobyl is in the grip of a wet nuclear winter. Here, Dr Nick

Tatopoulos (Matthew Broderick) is analysing the effects of nuclear contamination on earthworms and when called in to help with the Godzilla situation he is given the opportunity to provide the monster with a more specific biology than ever before. Based on his observations that the Chernobyl worms have grown 17 per cent bigger, and eventually tracking the monster's radiation traces back to French Polynesia, Tatopoulos is able to dismiss the 'lost dinosaur' theory and identify 'the dawn of a new species'. We even get a half-convincing reason why the monster chose New York: 'It's perfect. An island, water on all sides. But like no other island in the world he can easily hide'. This island theory partly explains why Godzilla chose New York rather than Los Angeles, for example. More will be said about the differences later, but the weather might also have something to do with it. In contrast to the volcanic West Coast, New York is in the grip of a particularly nasty storm. In effect it looks like Chernobyl, and there are certain instances when Godzilla seems to confound the storm. The main rains fall when the monster arrives, and his first triumphal bellow is accompanied by a lightning strike. What the storm also does is reverse evolution further by turning the island's inhabitants into fish. Having already destroyed the Japanese fishing trawlers, Godzilla lays into the harbour after being snagged on a fisherman's hook, and signals his arrival in Manhattan by hurling a boat onto the main street. The most specific choice of New York is revealed when the scientists work out that Godzilla is a 'she', a mutant Mother Nature looking for a suitable nesting place for its children-to-be.

Does size matter?

If there is a certain amount of continuity and justified development in terms of the monster and its change in context, the differences become much more apparent in the blockbusting mentality of the 1998 movie. Seen from this perspective, Dean Devlin and Roland Emmerich's *Godzilla* is not so much a remake of *Gojira* as another attempt at *Independence Day*, and furthermore trying to compete with all of the other disaster movies that had followed in that film's wake. As *Independence Day* and *Twister* demonstrate, the capabilities of recent cinema are such that disaster movies can be made more spectacular or more realistic than ever. What began with *Independence Day* and *Twister* in the summer of 1996, however, more or less ended in the summer of 1998 with *Godzilla* and *Armageddon*, and one of the reasons for this is that impressive, exaggerated scenes of destruction were quickly followed by similar, exaggerated scenes of destruction. It would be unfair to take *Independence Day*, *Deep Impact*, *Godzilla* and *Armageddon* to task for following their science fiction precepts through to exaggerated spectacle, but the problem lies in the fact that these science fiction disaster movies quickly became more or less indistinguishable from each other, the science fiction elements remaining consistent to a certain extent but the disasters decreasing in impact. This two-year flurry is in stark contrast to the ten-year reign, say, of similar science fiction disaster scenarios from the early 1950s through to the early 1960s.

While this is a criticism that could also be applied to the equally quick succession of natural disaster films like *Twister*, *Dante's Peak* and *Volcano*, it becomes particularly manifest in the science fiction disaster movies of the period. As *Independence Day* and, later, Tim Burton's *Mars Attacks!* (1996) had demonstrated, the fact that these films are based on long-familiar alien invasion and mutant monster movies is not necessarily the problem. Where *Mars Attacks!* bathed in ironic affection, one of the main pleasures of *Independence Day* was the way in which it did recycle overly-familiar science fiction scenarios with such energy and expertise. Following on from *Deep Impact*, *Armageddon* might well have been one more recycled asteroid movie too far (and in such quick succession), but *Godzilla* is as committed an old monster movie as *Independence Day* was an alien invasion B-movie with grade-A technicalities. It has become a common enough criticism of recent science fiction cinema to argue that only the special effects are special (see, for example, Pierson 1999). Although much less sympathetic than King Kong and regardless of nostalgic or retrospective 'cult' viewings of *Gojira*, this recent Godzilla and the film's scenes of destruction are much more impressive than the original 'man in a suit' lording it over a Lego-sized Tokyo like a Sumo wrestler. Which is to say that technical advances are not necessarily a bad thing, particularly where the attempt at successfully realising far-fetched scenes of destruction is concerned.

The allied but wider criticism of recent blockbusting cinema is that the advertising and merchandising have become much more important than the films themselves (see, for example, Dixon 1999). This is where contrasts become even more ingrained, but it is not so much that the industry surrounding *Godzilla* is vastly different to that which surrounded *Gojira* (the Japanese 'blockbuster' of its time) but that this attempt at a modern blockbuster gave the game away with its year-long 'Size Does Matter' campaign. Instead of contrasting old and new, comparisons between recent films become much more important in trying to assess the quick familiarity of a particular cycle of films. Here, Devlin and Emmerich were obviously keen to out-do their very successful, six-month 'ID4' campaign, but *Godzilla* followed this slow leak through to an interminable trickle. With the monster's foot first revealed in trailers accompanying *The Lost World: Jurassic Park* in 1997, the singular statement, 'Size Does Matter', was also designed to warn off impending competition. Surely it's what you do with it that counts.

Although *Godzilla* added a monster to the developing pattern of science fiction disaster movies, by the time the film came out it found itself located between two other films that were also destroying large portions of New York, and in a cycle which had already reached the point where the films were actually referring to each other. Just as *Independence Day* included a joke about the 'X-Files' television series, for example, *The X-Files* movie reciprocated by having somebody urinating on an old poster of *Independence Day* in an alleyway; and similarly, already wary of the 'Size Does Matter' campaign no doubt, *Armageddon* shows some Godzilla merchandise getting wiped out by its opening meteor shower. There are general narrative comparisons to be made between *Independence Day* and *Godzilla*: the initial widespread geography; the gradual approach to disaster; the main disaster sequences; a failed fight-back; a long period of holding back and hatching new plans; and then the protracted finale. Apart from being far less jingoistic and militaristic, what *Godzilla* does differently most of all, in terms of its narrative, is focus on just one of *Independence Day*'s main cities, but this makes it even more symptomatic in light of the other science fiction disaster movies of 1998.

In trying to come up with the largest disasters possible, the attractions of a city like New York are obvious, but in 1998 watching New York getting destroyed became standard fare. Disaster films have had a longstanding fascination with cities. From Babylon and Pompeii to Los Angeles and New York, cities have acted as material and symbolic centres of 'civilisation' and modernity. Principally, where cities thrive on construction, disaster films thrive on destruction. Focusing in particular on the history of the sky-scraper, Peter Wollen argues certain parallels with the growth of the modern metropolis and the development of film. With both beginning in the 1890s, the grand designs were established in the opening of the Woolworth build-ing in 1913 and the release of *The Birth of a Nation* in 1915, and then devel-oping to the 'classic' age of the New York skyscraper and the Hollywood studio system. There is, however, a fundamental 'ontological contradic-tion' (Wollen 1992: 25) between film and skyscrapers. Where skyscrapers are essentially vertical, film is essentially a horizontal form. This contra-diction leads to a positive collision when applied to disaster films. Far from accommodating cities, disaster films very literally work in cutting sky-scrapers down to size and levelling cities to the ground, the one twentieth-century technology in effect representing the destruction of another.

Over-populated and microcosmic, New York is the modern metropolis par excellence. Its skyline is instantly recognisable, the buildings proudly and arrogantly 'scraping' their identity into the very atmosphere. It could well be that the sheer familiarity of certain cities makes them the ideal target for disaster movies. It is in this sense, for example, that they enter into the shorthand geography of end-of-the-world films. So when *Inde-pendence Day* cuts to shots of Big Ben and the Kremlin, and *Armageddon* focuses in on the Eiffel Tower, the implications are that the destruction of a landmark is enough to symbolise the end of a city and extending to the invasion/destruction of an entire country. When *Godzilla*'s first shot of New York is accompanied by a caption – 'The city that never sleeps' – it is in part an attempt to avoid repetition (*Independence Day* had already introduced the city as 'New York') but it is also a label that, like 'The Big Apple', indi-cates both civic pride and tourist attraction. The former label denotes life and the latter size, the two main properties of this thriving city.

It could be argued that the 1998 version of *Godzilla* was totally justified in bringing the eponymous monster (back) to New York. *Gojira* had itself been influenced by two monster movies climaxing in the piecemeal destruction of New York, *King Kong* and *The Beast from 20,000 Fathoms*. King Kong climbing the newly constructed Empire State Building was a potent symbol of the primitive coming into contact with the modern, providing an iconic image that the 1976 remake failed to replace in its similar use of the World Trade Center. Where *The Beast From 20,000 Fathoms* signalled a slight return to New York, the majority of alien invasion and monster movies of the 1950s went for either small-town locations or Washington and Los Angeles, the country's political and entertainment capitals. For its part, the 1970s disaster cycle was a very Californian affair. Despite extending to the Midwest, transatlantic flights and Mediterranean cruises, New York remained relatively untouched.

As we have seen, where certain action movies had led the way in the 1990s, it was principally *Independence Day* which demonstrated the recent capabilities that can be brought to bear on spectacular scenes of metropolitan destruction. In featuring Los Angeles, Washington, New York, and identifiable postcard locations from around the world, *Independence Day* opened out a range of possibilities. Although *Deep Impact*, *Godzilla* and *Armageddon* followed the worldwide locations to a certain extent, they were much more centred on New York. With these films also leading their advertising campaigns with key shots of the city getting pummelled, while the attraction of destroying New York had became evident enough in *Independence Day* and possibly once more when the huge tidal wave hits in *Deep Impact*, by the time of the main smashing-of-New-York scenes in *Armageddon* and *Godzilla* the otherwise impressive effects had already become standard. As Tom Shone (1998: 4) stated in relation to the opening disaster sequence of *Armageddon*, 'it's the same old attraction we've been watching all summer long: the same loop tape of special effects showing cars flipping like cards, buildings shattering like meringues, and cities pockmarking with craters'.

Even the deliberate differences from *Independence Day* led *Armageddon* and *Godzilla* into similarity with each other. With *Independence Day* having already centred on the Empire State Building, for example, both feature the Chrysler building and Grand Central Station getting destroyed instead. *Godzilla* does focus on New York throughout, and this leads to protracted differences from *Independence Day* and *Armageddon* – not least, Godzilla is much more mobile and flexible than aliens and asteroids descending from out of the sky. But the other difference is the most symptomatic and that is the fact that it rains in *Godzilla*. This might be, as suggested earlier, in order to turn New York into a fish tank, but most of all it is a deliberate difference that points out the limited variations on offer. *Independence Day* destroyed New York on a clear night and lit it all up like a candle. *Deep Impact* and *Armageddon* showed it getting flooded and bombarded in the clear light of day. *Godzilla* has various parts of the city getting destroyed on a grey day into a dark night. It is in this sense that *Godzilla*'s use of the caption 'The city that never sleeps' also acts as an ironic commentary on over-use of the city in science fiction disaster movies of the time. Beset by aliens, asteroids and a roving monster, New Yorkers were to get very little sleep in the late 1990s.

4   SURVIVING DISASTER

Four of the top ten highest-grossing domestic films of 1998 were disaster movies. Of the films featured in Chapter 3, *Armageddon* reached second position ($201 million), *Deep Impact* seventh ($140 million) and *Godzilla* eighth ($136 million). By the following year, the brief intensive flurry of disaster movies sparked by *Independence Day* and *Twister* had clearly come to an end. Although elements of disaster featured in the combined *Jaws* and *Poseidon Adventure* action of *Deep Blue Sea* (1999), the Satanic *End of Days* (1999), and the romantic comedy *Forces of Nature* (1999), none of these films grossed the 'benchmark' blockbusting figure of $100 million (the most successful, *Deep Blue Sea*, earning $73 million and reaching 28th position). It would appear that, where the focus provided by disaster movies of the early 1970s led to complete standardisation over the course of a decade, the short-lived 1990s cycle did, indeed, reach saturation point in the summer of 1998. The importance of *Independence Day* and *Twister* in sparking this brief cycle is, however, marked by the fact that they still feature in the top twenty domestic grossers of all time, with the former at number nine ($306 million) and the latter at number eighteen ($241 million). What might seem so much commercial number-crunching is fundamental to identifying the popularity of certain trends and the principal movers and shakers in identifiable film cycles.

Most significant is the commercial success of James Cameron's *Titanic*. Released in December 1997, the film was the top US box-office earner of

1998 ($488 million) and, having garnered over $600 million overall, it replaced *Star Wars* to become the most successful film of all time. On one level, Cameron's film is as hybrid as the action and science fiction variants analysed in Chapters 2 and 3 but, even more so, it is a film that appears to belie simple, contemporary 'disaster movie' classification. That *Titanic* has been variously categorised as a romantic melodrama and an historical epic – classifications that have not been in regular use since the 1940s and 1950s – is also indicative of the film's historical generic scope. As reviews comparing it with *The Birth of a Nation*, *Gone with the Wind*, *Ben-Hur* (1959), *Lawrence of Arabia* (1962) and *Doctor Zhivago* (1965) indicate, one of the effects of the success of *Titanic* has been for film reviewers and academic critics alike to revisit the historical meaning of nothing less than the romance of spectacle (see Bernstein 1999: 22–5). As Diane Negra argues, however, the film also brings historical relevance into line with the present. So while *Titanic* might well have offered a refreshing change from the developing pattern of macho heroes facing up to, and ultimately winning out over, aliens and asteroids, this historical take on disaster is as resonant a millennial movie as any:

> *Titanic* sets itself in an analogous turn-of-the-century moment as an oblique means of interrogating current perceptions of economic, national, and technological fragility, and it suggests that our century began (as it might end) with disasters brought on by overly expansive human visions of technology in relation to creation. (1999: 220)

Where *Independence Day*, *Volcano* and the like make use of 1950s and 1970s precedents, the opportunity afforded by *Titanic* is to revisit and revise aspects of a wider cinematic history of disaster. We will begin by looking at *Titanic*'s status as a historical disaster film. While the narrative framework of the film is structured around the dramatisation of an actual historical event, by examining the film's use of representative characters, comparisons and contrasts with 1970s disaster movies can be drawn. We will end by looking at some of the ways in which the film can be identified as a definitive 1990s Hollywood product and the technological advances which distinguish it from 1970s disaster movies.

Delaying the inevitable

The innate advantage of James Cameron's *Titanic* is that it taps into a fascinating historical event which has become something of a modern mythology; its recurring themes being those of 'Golden Age' optimism giving way to feelings of insecurity and dread, new technology overextended, the simultaneous crystallisation and breakdown of hierarchical class distinctions, and the reminder that, above all, man is still regulated by Nature (see Howells 1999). The innate disadvantages, however, are that the history is so well known and that the subsequent mythology has much to do with the fact that the tale has been re-told so often. From the earliest surviving film version of the disaster, *Saved from the Titanic* (1912), through to numerous television productions such as *S.O.S. Titanic* (1979) and the 1996 miniseries *Titanic*, the events surrounding the sinking of the Titanic have provided for endless speculation and dramatisation. Characterised by a range of approaches, film versions of the disaster have progressed both in line with, and independent of, identifiable disaster cycles. One might point to David O. Selznick's film version that 'never was', for example, as a prime illustration of the attempt to bring the Titanic disaster into line with an existing disaster cycle: in this case, the historical disaster cycle of the late 1930s. Similarly, *Raise the Titanic!* (1980) acted as a fitting end to the 1970s disaster cycle, a film most notable for the fact that there is no disaster in it. For the most part, film versions of the Titanic disaster have taken place independently of the main disaster cycles. Hence, for example, the major film versions of the disaster, Herbert Selpin and Werner Klinger's Nazi propaganda piece, *Titanic* (1943), Jean Negulesco's star-studded Hollywood *Titanic* (1953) and Roy Ward Baker's classic British version, *A Night to Remember* (1958), all of which offer fascinating glimpses into the production values which could have been brought to bear on similar disaster films throughout the 1940s and 1950s (see Heyer 1995: 124–38).

The particular challenge of historical disaster films is to make the historically pre-determined as absorbing as possible, drawing audiences into the absolute certainty of disaster and following a variety of characters towards either death or survival. If the inevitable disasters depend upon how they are realised on film, these characters are key to maintaining our interest through to the fatal end. The main determinant of 'historical' disaster films, of course, is that they are set in the past. One of the resulting characteristics, however, is that, in contrast to the standard set by *The Poseidon Adventure*, they tend to end rather than begin with their disasters. While historical disaster films need not be restricted to actual historical disasters, for the most part they do make use of real-life situations. Yet even here, approaches vary from the wholly inaccurate *Krakatoa – East of Java* (Krakatoa, as many critics have pointed out, is actually west of Java) to the 'docudrama' framework adopted by *A Night to Remember*. Similarly, generic inflections range from the melodramatic approach of *San Francisco* to the speculative conspiracy mode adopted by *The Hindenburg*. Whereas previous film versions of the Titanic disaster had taken place solely in the past, Cameron's end-of-century version moves between the past and the present throughout. The film also combines several approaches, ranging from historical reconstruction and romance to epic/disaster/spectacle.

With its opening sepia shots of the launch of the ship, *Titanic* clearly establishes itself in the past. By then moving onto a present-day salvage mission with a hi-tech submergible floating over the wreck, the framework is such that the film attempts to span a whole mass of the Titanic legacy from the original disaster through to the resurgence in interest brought about by Robert Ballard's discovery of the wreck in 1985. While the film's opening scenes establish a sense of history as past, there is also something vaguely futuristic about the submergible as it hovers over the sea bed like a NASA capsule preparing to land on the moon. Cameron had already toyed with this idea of deep sea as outer space in *The Abyss* (1989), but here the wreck of the Titanic is established as a 'ghost ship' on a par with the Marie Celeste. The net is thus spread far and wide over history, mythology, documentary and reconstruction.

Cameron's principal focus, however, is provided by the film's frame narrative, wherein the century-old survivor, Rose Calvert (Gloria Stuart), tells Brock Lovett (Bill Paxton) and his salvage crew about her experiences of the disaster, in particular the shipboard romance between the young Rose (Kate Winslet) and Jack Dawson (Leonardo DiCaprio). The effects of this technique are such, therefore, that the history of the sinking of the Titanic is conveyed through a fictitious love story, the salvage crew in effect listening to the story as the cinema audience watches the film unfold.

While the film's frame narrative has a certain economy to it, providing the audience with plenty of initial exposition and allowing for focus throughout, the content of Rose's story is necessarily reductive and the form is such that, as well as being based on a disaster that is so well known, Cameron's *Titanic* also becomes the most narrated disaster film possible. As José Arroyo argues, Cameron's 'intimate epic' could have learnt a lot more from 1970s disaster movies in this respect:

> Such films ... began (like *Titanic*) by telling us of a situation that couldn't possibly happen, and introducing us to those it couldn't possibly happen to. Then – on as wide a screen as possible and preferably in Sensurround – they showed it happening: the eruption of a disaster and how different people coped. Unlike *Titanic*, however, the classic disaster movie introduced a wide array of characters, requiring star casting in order to facilitate characterisation. And always part of the fun was anticipating which stars would live and how the others met their grisly fates (doing Shelley Winters in *The Poseidon Adventure* is still a popular party piece). We need to care – or rather, to judge how well or badly these stars behaved in the crisis – in order that affect be generated. (1998: 18)

What is interesting here, of course, is that disaster movies of the 1970s are now being considered classics of the genre. What were often dismissed at the time as formulaic slaughter narratives with throwaway cardboard characters have at least gained some respect for being so unashamedly typical. But if not wholeheartedly praising 1970s disaster movies (they are only classics of their genre), Arroyo's contrast is as much to point out shortcomings in the affective narrative of *Titanic*. While the frame narrative effectively dissolves as the film progresses, we already know that Rose survives to tell the tale, for example. We might well be left wondering what will happen to Jack but, similarly, the salvage crew have got absolutely nothing to fear. With regard to the film's mix of fictional and factual passengers, for the most part the fictional characters are defined solely in relation to Rose and Jack (their opinions on the romance defining their characters) and, given that the factual characters have their fates written in history, anybody clued in to the Titanic disaster will already be aware that the Captain goes down with his ship and Molly Brown is unsinkable, for example.

Rather than referring to the emotional failings of *Titanic*, Arroyo is as much referring to the ingrained formula of disaster movies, wherein the 'fun' lies in following the characters through to death or survival, the interest lies in certain guessing-game expectations, and 'caring' about characters relates to 'judging' how they fare in the actual disaster. In disaster movies, fate is determined by ideology and the emotional becomes the judgemental. Where the characters in *Titanic* have been variously regarded as 'romance' and 'melodrama' types, they can, in fact, be regarded as 'disaster movie' types. In terms of actual historical figures, the film does follow the revisionist account of the disaster through to the characterisations to a certain degree but the inflections are recognisable from previous disaster movies. Here the previous scapegoats for the disaster, Captain Smith and designer Thomas Andrews, represent the decent middle ground and Bruce Ismay is the bureaucratic cad who gets to deliver the film's most hubristic soundbite: 'She is the largest moving object ever made by the hand of man in all history'. There is a sense in which Captain Smith is pulled along by a last blaze of glory but Ismay is very much the devil on his shoulder, telling him to stoke the ship up to its highest speed: 'This maiden voyage *must* make headlines'. Similarly, Andrews is far too confident about the 'strong and true' nature of the ship, and easily commanded, but as he explains to Rose there are only half the required number of lifeboats because it was 'thought … by some' that too many would clutter up the promenade. Both

Smith and Andrews are presented as bravely going down with their ship, and Ismay creeps his way into a lifeboat like the proverbial rat.

Certainly, there is a sense in which Cameron simplifies the rich/poor divide inherent in the upstairs/downstairs quality of the original ship even further, most obviously in the love story between 'tumbleweed' Jack and 'poor little rich girl' Rose. Again, the facts are that the rich did have open access to the promenade, the poor were crammed into steerage and the lifeboats were filled according to class. Within its own shorthand dramatisation of the inherent microcosmic divide, the film is quite successful in depicting the rich as arrogant and materialistic. This becomes most evident when Jack is invited to dinner after helping Rose. Prepared for the 'snake pit' by Molly Brown (Kathy Bates), Rose's fiancé and the main pantomime villain of the piece, Cal (Billy Zane), comments: 'Dawson? That's amazing, you could almost pass for a gentleman'. However, the contrast is much less successful down below. The poor remain as undefined as they were marginalised, the 'real party' downstairs imbued with much more life but with the various Italian, Russian and Irish immigrants presented as drinking and doing the Riverdance. Remaining indistinct on the whole, we are much more interested in seeing which of the upper-class characters will get their comeuppance. Whilst not altogether predictable in who lives and who dies, *Titanic* is in part reflecting the known facts. The reality of the disaster is such that the poor will perish and only a privileged few survive.

What distinguishes *Titanic*, most of all, with regard to its (issue-based) characterisations is its central heroine. This reflects what Alexandra Keller calls the film's 'virtual feminism' (1999: 143). This refers to Cameron's 'historical' take on the status of women – that is, the 1910s as seen from a 1990s perspective. The film makes it clear that what Rose is trying to free herself from are the social constraints of her time, the allied class reading being such that she is not only a woman, she is also a chattel. The most obvious retrospect is provided by the old Rose looking back on the situation, initially describing the Titanic as a 'slave ship' taking her back to America. This is echoed in the young Rose comparing her relationship to Cal in terms of master and slave: 'I'm not a foreman in one of your mills that you can command!'. As Rose's Victorian mother explains, this is a marriage of convenience and finance, necessitated by the fact that they have inherited 'a legacy of bad debts hidden by a good name'..The marriage is for the sake of the family's standing in society: 'Of course it's unfair, we're the women. Our choices are never easy'. It is principally when the iceberg hits and *Titanic* slips into action movie mode, however, that Cameron lets his anachronisms run riot. Particularly in the scene where Rose rescues Jack with an axe, she becomes the suffragette version of Cameron's science fiction heroines, Ripley in *Aliens* (1986) and Sarah Connor in *The Terminator* (1984) and *Terminator 2* (1991) (see Kramer 1999; Lubin 1999: 79–85). Although an obvious 1990s take on the 'New Woman' of the 1910s, Kate Winslet's Rose is that previously rare thing, an active disaster movie heroine. Karen Black's role in *Airport 1975* is the exception to the masculine rule with regard to the 1970s disaster cycle, but strong heroines have featured in a number of recent disaster movies; principally, for example, Helen Hunt in *Twister*, Anne Heche in *Volcano* and Tea Leoni in *Deep Impact*.

Disaster and spectacle

In trying to isolate reasons 'Why People the World Over Have Spent Two Hours and Seventy-four Minutes Watching a Boat Sink ...', Alexandra Keller begins by introducing *Titanic* as an all-in-one package, 'a stunningly executed, special-effects-laden, working-class-loving, owning-class-hating, strong-willed-heroine-driven, romantic tragedy that ... almost doubled as a swashbuckling sea picture'. Where other suggestions follow (Cameron's special effects, DiCaprio's sex appeal), Keller admits her own reason: '*I* went to see what the most expensive movie in the world looked like' (1999: 132). The fact that *Titanic* emerged as the most expensive and most profitable film of all time has led to many considerations of the film's 'commercial meaning'. Firstly, this refers to the film's status as both 'text' and 'product' – which is to say that considerations of *Titanic*'s historical framework, disaster narrative and class/gender characterisations, as outlined in the previous section, lend themselves well to accounting for the film's popularity. If this refers to the film's status as both text and product, *Titanic* has been used to isolate a number of industrial strategies that emphasise the film's status as an altogether widespread commercial product, including merchandising, advertising and mass media coverage. Rather than looking at the numerous reasons why *Titanic* became the most successful film of all time, I would like to end by looking at the ways in which it works as a disaster spectacle (in effect, making it the most successful disaster film of all time).

It would be very easy to dismiss *Titanic* as cold-hearted technological romanticism or claim that its appeal was entirely mass manufactured. This is certainly Wheeler Dixon's view in *Disaster and Memory: Celebrity Culture and the Crisis of Hollywood Cinema* (1999). Here, Dixon looks at the ways in which disaster is being increasingly presented by the media as a form of entertainment. Whether this is looked at in terms of films or news coverage, the point is that it is becoming increasingly difficult to tell the difference between the two. The controversy surrounding David Cronenberg's *Crash* (1996), an adaptation of J. G. Ballard's supposed disaster porn novel, is one of Dixon's main examples, and even more so in his extended analysis of the mass of reporting surrounding the death of Princess Diana in 1997. While Dixon is at times genuinely disturbed at the ways in which Diana's death quickly became little more than a profitable news story, the success of *Titanic* is even more readily attributed to all of the key production and marketing strategies of the 'Dominant Cinema'. If the reality of Diana's death led to a whole network of media practices and an altogether complex mixing of emotions, the singular trick of *Titanic* a few months later was to draw audiences in with romance, disaster, and spectacle.

In his subsequent attack on *Titanic* and overview of disaster films, Dixon develops a number of useful prejudices. In looking on Cameron's film as a sort of cyborg remake of *A Night to Remember*, Dixon states: 'Unlike Baker's film ... Cameron's *Titanic* offers spectacle in the place of substance and cynically attempts to capture the audience's attention through the use of an archetypal Romeo and Juliet "star-cross'd lovers" conceit' (Dixon 1999: 3). The familiar argument here is that of spectacle over substance, with *Titanic* in effect trying and failing to make up for its emotional deficiencies through use of a hackneyed love story. Following on from similar comparisons between *Earth vs the Flying Saucers* and *Independence Day*, Dixon goes on to raise the second familiar argument, one that might be termed 'economics' over 'ingenuity'. As he claims, 'numerous other disaster films of the fifties, sixties, and seventies brought about the destruction of cities, countries, and even entire civilizations in a compellingly low-budget manner' (p. 4). This may well be true in the case of 1950s and 1960s science fiction B-movies but certainly not in the case of 1970s disaster movies. After a brief consideration of *The Towering Inferno*, Dixon concludes:

> All these films were created for comparatively little money; almost without exception, their special effects … have become dated and unconvincing with the passage of time, and the increasing reliance on digital effects. But though technology continues to evolve, the disaster film continues to thrive in ever-more-rarefied territory, the cost of production driven up into the $50–90 million range through the demands of increased star salaries, lavish sequences of destruction, and international ad campaigns. (pp. 5–6)

There is, of course, a nostalgic sense of 'they don't make 'em like that any more' in Dixon's account. In order to balance out the retrospect, one might point out that, for its time, the $1 million *A Night to Remember* was a major commercial undertaking. With star names reduced to mere cameos, the film's emotional involvement principally relates to its focus on the ship's officers retaining a stiff upper lip when the iceberg hits (see, for example, Lubin 1999: 76–7). Similarly, what Dixon also seems to forget is that films like *The Towering Inferno* were at the very forefront of New Hollywood economics.

In an industry that spends almost as much time and money in promoting its seasonal blockbusters as it does in getting them made, the scope moves far beyond the films themselves. With specific regard to the two main arguments mentioned above, let us focus on *Titanic*'s final hour: the film's representation and dramatisation of disaster. Where 'representation' can easily fall into the argument of aesthetics and experience over narrative drive and character development, 'dramatisation' refers to the ways

FIGURE 7 *Titanic: The Love Boat*

in which the film's potentially overwhelming climax both adds to and completes everything that has gone before it in a spectacular and, above all, effective manner. One of the most notable features of *Titanic* is its use of computer-generated imaging (CGI). This is one of the defining characteristics of the 1990s disaster cycle as a whole, from the distinctive 'photorealistic' tornadoes in *Twister* to the repetitive scenes of mass destruction in *Godzilla* and *Armageddon*. Recent analyses of new special-effects technologies have worked in locating the latest innovations within a wider history of cinema as technology and defending what has often been dismissed as the most cosmetic aspect of contemporary film-making. Or, putting the two together, that history is also part of the defence, the argument being that contemporary special-effects technologies represent the next justified step in a longstanding and ongoing cinema of spectacle (see, for example, Cook and Bernink 1999: 45–64). The current, computer-generated revolution has had its most obvious breakthroughs in science fiction and fantasy films (see Pierson 1999). In his survey of technological developments from widescreen to CGI, Michael Allen argues: 'The drive behind much of the technical development in cinema since 1950 has been towards both a greater or heightened sense of 'realism' and a bigger, more breathtaking realization of spectacle' (1998: 127). It is in this wider sense – technology as representation and cinema as experience – that CGI has also worked through historical simulation and spectacle, from key battle sequences in *Saving Private Ryan* (1998) and *The Patriot* (2000) to the overall historical settings and battle sequences in *Gladiator* (2000) and *Pearl Harbour* (2001).

Characteristic of most writing on the subject, there is a distinction to make, first of all, between visual and special effects. Visual effects are 'invisible' and often background effects, special effects become most apparent during key action sequences. The liquid morphing effects in Cameron's previous films, *The Abyss* and *Terminator 2: Judgment Day*, for example, were special effects used in relation to the films' respective shape-shifting alien and cyborg entities. Watching *Titanic* we are not necessarily meant to register the fact that the computer-generated ship sails a computer-generated sea. There are times, however, when the ship first sets sail and, most noticeably, when the ship goes down, that movement, perspective and action work in turning simulation into spectacle – or, we become too involved in the experience to register the fact that what we are seeing are special effects. Where criticisms follow with regard to special

effects bringing about 'the death of narrative' (Barker 2000: 170), detract-
ing from character development and emotional involvement, it could be
argued, in the first instance, that the main 'character' – or at least element
– introduced and developed through the film's overall production values
is the ship itself. This is to say that in the first two hours of the film we
are given a lot more insight into the workings and majesty of the object of
disaster than any other plane, ship or building before. The ship itself is,
indeed, well characterised in this respect. If the passengers do walk around
like mannequin representatives of their class to a certain extent, this is
because they are dwarfed by a ship which says it all in the first place – the
magnificent ballroom in contrast to the tight corridors below or the high
perch of the cockpit aloof from the hellish engine room. Filmed on a 90 per
cent replica of the ship and in the studio, if this points the ship's physical
existence as an actual set, the film's visual and special effects effectively
bring the ship to life through the combination of live action, model shots
and CGI. On one level the ship remains a material reminder of society, but
in intermediate shots we see the ship speeding away and in long shots it
becomes a mere isolated object. From launch to disaster we are on a journey with the ship itself, by turns a lavish set and a convincing, hazy computer-generated illusion carried along by the perceived context of movement.

In terms of the disaster itself, the leisurely splendour of the journey
is certainly matched and outstripped by the final hour of the film. This is
the predetermined culmination of the film, and with more specific narrative elements developed and resolved through the very action of the disaster. The most curious crossover of fact and fiction at this point is that,
having consummated their relationship and run onto the deck to escape
Cal's men, Jack and Rose kiss and then the iceberg hits. At the very point
at which Rose commits herself to running away with Jack, this small breaking of the shackles which bind her to conventional society is matched by
the iceberg smashing into the side of the ship. It is a cheeky metaphorical
moment compounded by the very specific indication that the lookouts are
so distracted by the lovers that they fail to spot the iceberg in time. Or,
boiling the suggestive and the particular down to the bare narrative essentials, Jack and Rose are the cause of the disaster. From this point on, both

the fictional love story and the actual sinking provide for both narrative urgency and the spectacular representation of disaster. The actual facts of the disaster are that the ship did take one hour to go down and the film is almost 'real time' in its subsequent pacing, slow and almost imperceptible at first but with the speed increasing as the ship fills with water. The narrative gap is such that whereas *The Poseidon Adventure* followed its two-minute disaster sequence through to over an hour's worth of survival, the protracted sinking of the Titanic is such that disaster is combined with attempts at survival. As José Arroyo finally admits: 'Only with death imminent does everything come to life. Characters shake loose, scenes finally begin to play and drama to happen as the chaos commences' (1998: 16).

Principally, the action is such that while Jack and Rose strive to save each other and help others along the way, Cal tries to split them apart and finally settles for grabbing a baby in order to get on a lifeboat reserved for women and children. While the 'money's worth' reading of the film may not care too much about the characters, there is little denying the power of the 'money shot' when the ship finally breaks in two, the decks splintering and the funnels falling. As the bottom half of the ship goes under, the top half is flipped up 90 degrees. Jack and Rose scramble to the top of the upturned bow (the place where they first met), and the camera rises vertically above them. The top half is finally pulled straight down and we ride down with it and them into the cold, seething sea. As David Lubin argues, in its representation of an actual historical disaster, *Titanic* can also be said to have reproduced certain historical, cinematic effects, taking people back to the experience of how audiences might well have responded to epic disaster spectacles of the time like *Quo Vadis?*, *The Last Days of Pompeii* and *Cabiria*. In an age in which disasters and disaster movies have become commonplace, *Titanic* finally escapes comparisons with the likes of *The Poseidon Adventure* and *The Towering Inferno*: 'in none of those films was mass death envisioned as graphically, convincingly and seriously as here' (Lubin 1999: 112). In its combination of action, peril and attempts at survival, the climax of *Titanic* is certainly one of the most sustained of all disaster sequences.

After the deluge

Titanic can be located as both part of, and simultaneously independent of, the late 1990s disaster cycle. With its focus on history and romance, for example, the film is in pointed contrast to the likes of *Independence Day*, *Twister, Volcano* and *Armageddon*. While James Cameron had been developing ideas for a *Titanic* movie for over five years, however, the project was only given the specific go-ahead after the success of *Independence Day* and *Twister*, both of which not only demonstrated that the technological capabilities were in place for such an undertaking but also that there was a definite appetite for disaster. The phenomenal success of *Titanic* would also have an effect on subsequent disaster movies, which is to say that in the 'post-*Titanic*' summer of 1998, while films like *Deep Impact* and *Armageddon* were very successful, in relative terms, of course, they were much less profitable than Cameron's 'ship of dreams' (see Keller 1999).

In combining history and disaster, *Titanic* was a financial risk that came to succeed in exactly the right ways at the right time. As *Independence Day* and *Twister* had led the way with regard to 'natural' and 'science fiction' disaster movies, one would have thought that *Titanic* might have gone on to inspire a similar wave of historical disaster films. With disaster movies declining in relative value, however, the nearest equivalents to *Titanic* have been *Gladiator* and *Pearl Harbour*, both of which represent similar computer-generated resurrections of historical genres. In a manner not at all dissimilar to the 1970s disaster cycle, the most immediate legacy of *Twister*, *Volcano, Deep Impact, Armageddon* and the like was a number of television movies. The points raised about repetition at the end of Chapter 3 become even more apparent in television productions such as *Tornado!* (1996), *Night of the Twisters* (1996), *Asteroid* (1996), *Volcano: Fire on the Mountain* (1997), *Eruption* (1997), *Doomsday Rock* (1997), *Meteorites!* (1997), *Storm Chasers: The Revenge of the Twister* (1998) and then progressing onto the obvious combination that cinema never got round to, *Earthquake in Manhattan* (1998) and *Aftershocks: Earthquake in New York* (1999). The end of the millennium has a lot to answer for.

It looks likely that after such a concentrated and crossbreed flurry of activity, 'disaster movies' will now sit back and let 'disaster' take over again. On one level this refers to the fact that elements of disaster have remained a pervasive feature of action and science fiction cinema. Part of the failure of *Battlefield Earth* (2000), for example, could be ascribed to the fact that whereas *Independence Day* worked its way towards averting apocalypse after disaster, what was initially trumpeted as an *ID4* for the new millennium proceeds with a fight-back that can only partly reverse the effects of the film's prior, catastrophic, alien invasion. Conversely, part of the success of *Mission: Impossible 2* (2000) could be related to its race-against-time action, wherein Tom Cruise tries to avert the release of a deadly virus. Although separated by six months, 2000's main 'duelling movies' provide for an interesting perspective whereby survival and rescue have been brought to the fore: in part carrying on where *Apollo 13* (1995) left off, *Mission to Mars* and *Red Planet* centre on attempts to rescue stranded astronauts. This theme was also developed in *Space Cowboys* later the same year, wherein an attempt to repair a falling satellite leads to the astronauts having to save themselves. Principally, in the 1990s, disaster movies wallowed in disasters that were not followed through to the cataclysmic end. Now that we have survived all of those films and the end of the world has not happened, perhaps survival narratives are the natural result. As Diane Negra argues, for all their catastrophic scenes of death and destruction, disaster movies are ultimately about 'disaster readiness'. As particularly evident in the late 1990s, such films end with images of rescue, redemption, reconstruction and reassertion, at both personal levels (Rose surviving the sinking of the Titanic) and on national and global scales (all-American heroes saving the world). They are, above all, survivalist texts (Negra 1999: 233–5).

The theme of survival has emerged in a number of films that begin with disastrous circumstances, for example the plane crashes leaving the protagonists stranded on desert islands in the romantic comedy *Six Days, Seven Nights* (1998) and the Robinson Crusoe drama *Cast Away* (2000). Beginning with a train disaster and playing off the tensions between its doom-laden 'glass man' and an unsuspecting superhero, *Unbreakable*

(2000) says a lot about modern obsessions with disaster and the need to believe in survival. Whereas elements of disaster have featured in a number of recent films, two much more specific and identifiable disaster/survival movies emerged in 2000, in the form of *The Perfect Storm* and *Vertical Limit*. Whereas the latter goes for a *Cliffhanger* (1993) approach to its mountaineering subject, *The Perfect Storm* was much more successful in its use and adaptation of familiar disaster movie elements. Based on Sebastian Junger's best-selling account of the sinking of a fishing trawler off the coast of Massachusetts in 1991, the film itself goes for the 'slow burn' approach, the first half devoted to the Gloucester community and the second half devoted to the main fishermen at sea and the developing storm. Following the recent tendency (as exemplified by *Titanic* and *Deep Impact*) of deferring its developing disaster until the second half of the film, the enduring image, of course, is of the finale – the trawler riding halfway up a hundred-foot wave. Using this as the climactic shot of the film's trailer and the image crystallised on its poster, there is no doubt that *The Perfect Storm* marketed itself as a disaster movie. That the film was based on a relatively recent, real-life event also led to interest in the film itself. This was not only part of the film's advertising but also the subject of not inconsiderable debate regarding dramatic license (principally, how can anyone know exactly what happened to the fishermen in that fateful storm?). Where *Titanic* had led the way with regard to the historical blurring of fact and fiction, the relatively recent setting of *The Perfect Storm* added particular fuel to a debate which has already, in part, gone on to inform the production of the provisionally titled *K-19: The Widowmaker*. Although based on the incidents surrounding the Russian nuclear submarine that suffered a radiation leak in the North Atlantic in 1961, the film began production not long after the sinking of the Kursk in 2000. It remains to be seen whether such 'localised' disaster dramas will go on to constitute a general trend in the forthcoming years; that is, films based on very specific incidents or situations and offering a fundamental shift away from the concentrated flurry of 'metropolitan' disaster movies produced in the late 1990s. In blurring the distinction between fact and fiction, certainly such films act as a reminder that disasters can happen anywhere and at any time. Yet principally, like all disaster movies, they should also work in reassuring us that disasters take place in exceptional circumstances.

FILMOGRAPHY

The Abyss (James Cameron, 1989, US)
Accidental Hero (Stephen Frears, 1992, US)
Aftershocks: Earthquake in New York (Mikael Salomon, 1999, US)
Air Force One (Wolfgang Petersen, 1997, US)
Airplane (Jim Abrahams, David Zucker, 1980, US)
Airport (George Seaton, 1970, US)
Airport 1975 (Jack Smight, 1974, US)
Airport '77 (Jerry Jameson, 1977, US)
Aliens (James Cameron, 1986, US)
Alive (Frank Marshall, 1992, US)
Alphaville (Jean-Luc Godard, 1965, Fr./It.)
A Night to Remember (Roy Ward Baker, 1958, UK)
Apollo 13 (Ron Howard, 1995, US)
Arlington Road (Mark Pellington, 1998, US)
Armageddon (Michael Bay, 1998, US)
Asteroid (Bradford May, 1996, US)
Atlantis (G. W. Pabst, 1932, Ger.)
Avalanche (Corey Allen, 1978, US)
Backdraft (Ron Howard, 1991, US)
Batman Forever (Joel Schumacher, 1995, US)
Battlefield Earth (Roger Christian, 2000, US)
Battle in the Clouds (Walter Booth, 1909, US)
The Beast from 20,000 Fathoms (Eugène Lourié, 1953, US)
The Bedford Incident (James B. Harris, 1965, UK)
Ben-Hur (Fred Niblo, 1925, US)
Ben-Hur (William Wyler, Andrew Marton, 1959, US)
Beyond the Poseidon Adventure (Irwin Allen, 1979, US)
The Big Bus (James Frawley, 1976, US)
The Birds (Alfred Hitchcock, 1963, US)

The Birth of a Nation (D. W. Griffith, 1915, US)
The Blob (Irvin S. Yeaworth Jr, 1958, US)
Blown Away (Stephen Hopkins, 1994, US)
Bonnie and Clyde (Arthur Penn, 1967, US)
Bullitt (Peter Yates, 1968, US)
Cabiria (Giovanni Pastrone, 1914, It.)
The Cassandra Crossing (George Pan Cosmatos, 1976, UK/It./Ger.)
Cast Away (Robert Zemeckis, 2000, US)
The Catastrophe of the Balloon 'Le Pax' (Georges Méliès, 1902, Fr.)
Cliffhanger (Renny Harlin, 1993, US)
Close Encounters of the Third Kind (Steven Spielberg, 1977, US)
Collision and Shipwreck at Sea (Georges Méliès, 1898, Fr.)
Con Air (Simon West, 1997, US)
The Concorde – Airport '79 (David Lowell Rich, 1979, US)
Cool Hand Luke (Stuart Rosenberg, 1967, US)
Crash (David Cronenberg, 1996, Can.)
The Creature from the Black Lagoon (Jack Arnold, 1954, US)
Dante's Peak (Roger Donaldson, 1997, US)
The Day the Earth Stood Still (Robert Wise, 1951, US)
Deep Blue Sea (Renny Harlin, 1999, US)
Deep Impact (Mimi Leder, 1998, US)
The Detective (Gordon Douglas, 1968, US)
Detour to Terror (Michael O'Herlihy, 1980, US)
Die Hard (John McTiernan, 1988, US)
Die Hard 2 (Renny Harlin, 1990, US)
Die Hard with a Vengeance (John McTiernan, 1995, US)
Dirty Harry (Don Siegel, 1971, US)
Doctor Zhivago (David Lean, 1965, US)
Dr Strangelove; or, How I Learned to Stop Worrying and Love the Bomb
     (Stanley Kubrick, 1963,UK)
Doomsday Rock (Brian Trenchard-Smith, 1997, US)
Easy Rider (Dennis Hopper, 1969, US)
Earth vs the Flying Saucers (Fred F. Sears, 1956, US)
Earthquake (Mark Robson, 1974, US)
Earthquake in Manhattan (Terry Ingram, 1998, US)
End of Days (Peter Hyams, 1999, US)
End of the World (Abel Gance, 1930, Fr.)
Eruption (Gwyneth Gibby, 1997, US)
The Eruption of Mount Pelée (Georges Méliès, 1902, Fr.)
Executive Decision (Stuart Baird, 1996, US)
Fail Safe (Sidney Lumet, 1964, US)
The Fall of the Roman Empire (Anthony Mann, 1964, US/Sp.)
The Fall of Troy (Giovanni Pastrone, 1914, It.)
Fearless (Peter Weir, 1993, US)

Flame of the Barbary Coast (Joseph Kane, 1945, US)
Forces of Nature (Bronwen Hughes, 1999, US)
48 Hours (Walter Hill, 1982, US)
The French Connection (William Friedkin, 1971, US)
Gladiator (Ridley Scott, 2000, US)
Godzilla (Roland Emmerich, 1998, US)
Godzilla, King of the Monsters (Ishiro Honda, Terry O. Morse, 1956, US/Jap.)
Gojira (Inoshiro Honda, 1954, Jap.)
Gone with the Wind (Victor Fleming, George Cukor, Sam Wood, 1939, US)
The Great Escape (John Sturges, 1963, US)
Hard Rain (Mikael Salomon, 1998, US)
The High and the Mighty (William Wellman, 1954, US)
The Hindenburg (Robert Wise, 1975, US)
The Hurricane (John Ford, 1937, US)
Independence Day (Roland Emmerich, 1996, US)
In Old Chicago (Henry King, 1938, US)
Interrupted Honeymoon, The (Georges Méliès, 1899, Fr.)
Intolerance (D. W. Griffith, 1916, US)
Invasion of the Body Snatchers (Don Siegel, 1955, US)
Jaws (Steven Spielberg, 1975, US)
Juggernaut (Richard Lester, 1974, UK)
King Kong (Merian C. Cooper, Ernest Schoedsack, 1933, US)
King Kong (John Guillerman, 1976, US)
King of Kings (Cecil B. DeMille, 1927, US)
Krakatoa – East of Java (Bernard Kowalski, 1968, US)
The Last Days of Pompeii (Luigi Maggi, 1908, It.)
The Last Days of Pompeii (Mario Caserini, 1913, It.)
The Last Days of Pompeii (Carmine Gallone, 1926, It.)
The Last Days of Pompeii (Ernest B. Schoedsack, 1935, US)
Lawrence of Arabia (David Lean, 1962, UK)
Lethal Weapon (Richard Donner, 1987, US)
The Longest Day (Andrew Marton, Ken Annakin, Bernhard Wicks, 1962, US)
The Lost World (Harry O. Hoyt, 1925, US)
The Lost World: Jurassic Park (Steven Spielberg, 1997, US)
Mars Attacks! (Tim Burton, 1996, US)
Meteor (Ronald Neame, 1979, US)
Meteorites! (Chris Thompson, 1997, US)
Metropolis (Fritz Lang, 1926, Ger.)
Midway (Jack Smight, 1976, US)
The Misfortunes of an Explorer (Georges Méliès, 1900, Fr.)
Mission: Impossible (Brian De Palma, 1996, US)
Mission: Impossible 2 (John Woo, 2000, US)
Mission to Mars (Brian De Palma, 2000, US)
The Naked Jungle (Byron Haskin, 1954, US)

Night of the Twisters (Timothy Bond, 1996, US)
No Highway in the Sky (Henry Koster, 1951, US)
Noah's Ark (Michael Curtiz, 1929, US)
The Omega Man (Boris Sagal, 1971, US)
Outbreak (Wolfgang Petersen, 1995, US)
Passenger 57 (Kevin Hooks, 1992, US)
The Patriot (Roland Emmerich, 2000, US)
The Peacemaker (Mimi Leder, 1997, US)
Pearl Harbour (Michael Bay, 2001, US)
The Perfect Storm (Wolfgang Petersen, 2000, US)
Phase IV (Saul Bass, 1973, UK)
Piranha (Joe Dante, 1978, US)
Planet of the Apes (Franklin Schaffner, 1968, US)
The Poseidon Adventure (Ronald Neame, 1972, US)
Quo Vadis? (Enrico Guazzoni, 1912, It.)
Quo Vadis? (Arturo Ambrosio, 1924, It.)
Quo Vadis? (Mervyn Le Roy, 1951, US)
Raiders of the Lost Ark (Steven Spielberg, 1981, US)
The Rains Came (Clarence Brown, 1939, US)
Raise the Titanic! (Jerry Jameson, 1980, US)
Random Hearts (Sydney Pollack, 1999, US)
Red Planet (Antony Hoffman, 2000, US)
The Rock (Michael Bay, 1996, US)
Rocky (John G. Avildsen, 1976, US)
Rollercoaster (James Goldstone, 1977, US)
San Francisco (W. S. Van Dyke, 1936, US)
Saved from the Titanic (Étienne Arnaud, 1912, US)
Saving Private Ryan (Steven Spielberg, 1998, US)
The Siege (Edward Zwick, 1998, US)
Sign of the Cross (Cecil B. DeMille, 1932, US)
Six Days, Seven Nights (Ivan Reitman, 1998, US)
S.O.S. Titanic (William Hale, 1979, US)
Soylent Green (Richard Fleischer, 1973, US)
Speed (Jan de Bont, 1994, US)
Speed 2: Cruise Control (Jan de Bont, 1997, US)
Squirm (Jeff Lieberman, 1976, US)
Stagecoach (John Ford, 1939, US)
Star Trek: The Motion Picture (Robert Wise, 1979, US)
Star Wars (George Lucas, 1977, US)
Storm Chasers: Revenge of the Twister (Mark Sobel, 1998, US)
Sudden Death (Peter Hyams, 1995, US)
Suez (Allan Dwan, 1938, US)
Superman (Richard Donner, 1978, US/UK)
The Swarm (Irwin Allen, 1978, US)

The Ten Commandments (Cecil B. DeMille, 1923, US)
The Ten Commandments (Cecil B. DeMille, 1956, US)
Tentacles (Oliver Hellman, 1976, It./US)
The Terminator (James Cameron, 1984, US)
Terminator 2: Judgment Day (James Cameron, 1991, US)
Them! (Gordon Douglas, 1954, US)
The Thing (Christian Nyby, 1951, US)
Things to Come (William Cameron Menzies, 1936, UK)
Titanic (Herbert Selpin and Werner Klinger, 1943, Ger.)
Titanic (Jean Negulesco, 1953, US)
Titanic (James Cameron, 1997, US)
Top Gun (Tony Scott, 1986, US)
Tornado! (Noel Nosseck, 1996, US)
The Towering Inferno (John Guillermin, Irwin Allen, 1974, US)
Transatlantic Tunnel (Maurice Elvey, 1935, UK)
Turbulence (Robert Butler, 1997, US)
Twelve Monkeys (Terry Gilliam, 1995, US)
20,000 Leagues Under the Sea (Richard Fleischer, 1954, US)
Twister (Jan de Bont, 1996, US)
Unbreakable (M. Night Shyamalan, 2000, US)
Under Siege (Andrew Davis, 1992, US)
Under Siege 2: Dark Territory (Geoff Murphy, 1995, US)
Vertical Limit (Martin Campbell, 2000, US)
Volcano (William Dieterle, 1953, It.)
Volcano (Mick Jackson, 1997, US)
Volcano: Fire on the Mountain (Graeme Campbell, 1997, US)
War of the Worlds, The (Byron Haskin, 1953, US)
Waterworld (Kevin Reynolds, 1995, US)
When Time Ran Out (James Goldstone, 1980, US)
When Worlds Collide (Rudolph Maté, 1951, US)
The Wizard of Oz (Victor Fleming, 1939, US)
X the Unknown (Leslie Norman, 1956, UK)
X-Files: Fight the Future, The (Rob Bowman, 1998, US)
Zardoz (John Boorman, 1974, UK)
Zeppelin (Etienne Périer, 1971, US)

BIBLIOGRAPHY

Allen, M. (1998) 'From *Bwana Devil* to *Batman Forever*: Technology in Contemporary Hollywood
   Cinema', in S. Neale and M. Smith (eds) *Contemporary Hollywood Cinema*. London and New
   York: Routledge, 109–29.
   A useful account of technological developments from widescreen to CGI.
Altman, R. (1999) *Film/Genre*. London: BFI.
   An extensive survey and re-evaluation of genre criticism.
Annan, D. (1975) *Catastrophe: The End of the Cinema?* New York: Bounty Books.
   Mainly illustrative but with some very good details about the history of the disaster genre.
Arroyo, J. (1998) 'Massive Attack', *Sight and Sound*, 8, 2, 16–19.
   James Cameron's Titanic in the context of recent action/spectacle cinema.
_____ (2000) (ed.) *Action/Spectacle Cinema: A Sight and Sound Reader*. London: BFI.
   A variety of articles and reviews on recent action/spectacle cinema.
Babington, B. and P. W. Evans (1993) *Biblical Epics: Sacred Narrative in the Hollywood Cinema*.
   Manchester: Manchester University Press.
   *A useful introduction to biblical epics with several arguments relating to disaster and
   spectacle.*
Balio, T. (1993) *Grand Design: Hollywood as a Modern Business Enterprise, 1930–1939*. New
   York: Scribner's.
   An extensive analysis of production trends in the 1930s.
Barker, M. (2000) *From Antz to Titanic: Reinventing Film Analysis*. London: Pluto.
   Contains useful chapters on Deep Impact and Titanic.
Barkun, M. (1974) *Disaster and the Millennium*. New Haven and London: Yale University Press.
   A wide-ranging account of disaster and millenarianism.
Benjamin, M. (1998) *Living at the End of the World*. London: Macmillan.
   Historical perspectives on the end of the world, from the Book of Revelation to Waco.
Bernstein, M. (1999) "Floating Triumphantly': The American Critics on *Titanic*', in K. S. Sandler
   and G. Studlar (eds) *Titanic: Anatomy of a Blockbuster*. New Brunswick, New Jersey: Rutgers
   University Press, 14–28.

A survey of Titanic reviews with particular emphasis on comparisons with epics.

Cook, P. and M. Bernink (eds) (1999) *The Cinema Book* (2nd edn.). London: BFI.

An extremely useful guide to historical and contemporary approaches to film. Very good, in particular, on genre, technology and the New Hollywood.

Cubitt, S. (1999) '*Le reel, c'est l'impossible*: the sublime time of special effects', *Sight and Sound*, 9, 7, 123–30.

Introduction to a special edition of Sight and Sound devoted to recent special effects technologies.

Davis, M. (1999) *Ecology of Fear: Los Angeles and the Imagination of Disaster*. New York: Vintage.

Riot, earthquakes, floods and fire in the City of Angels. Particularly good on LA-based disaster movies as a form of 'denial'.

Dixon, W. W. (1999) *Disaster and Memory: Celebrity Culture and the Crisis of Hollywood Cinema*. New York: Columbia University Press.

A polemical account of the current state of the 'Dominant Cinema', in particular focusing on disaster as represented in film and by the media.

Drosnin, M. (1997) *The Bible Code*. London: Orion.

Best-selling millennial merchandise. A whole history of disaster as mathematically encoded in the Bible, with the final end of the world predicted for 2006, 2010 or 2012 …

Durgnat, R. (1977) 'Epic, Epic, Epic, Epic, Epic', in B. K. Grant (ed.) *Film Genre: Theory and Criticism*. Metuchen, New Jersey and London: Scarecrow Press, 108–17.

Particularly good on biblical and Roman epics.

Dyer, R. (1975) 'American Cinema in the '70s: *The Towering Inferno*', *Movie*, 21, 30–3.

Succinct analysis of the film's appeal, particularly focusing on its use of stars.

_____ (1998) *Stars: New Edition*. London: BFI.

Updated version of Dyer's 1979 classic, with a supplementary chapter by Paul McDonald.

Freer, I. (1998) 'Hard Rock Cachet', *Empire*, 108, 98–103.

An account of Deep Impact in the context of 'millennial madness', scientific observations of approaching asteroids and the impending competition of Armageddon.

Gertner, R. (1970) '*Airport*', *Motion Picture Herald*, 240, 8, 379.

Airport as good old-fashioned entertainment.

Gross, L. (1995) 'Big and Loud', *Sight and Sound*, 5, 8, 7–10.

Succinct account and defence of action movies. Features some very good comparisons with disaster movies.

Heyer, P. (1995) *Titanic Legacy: Disaster as Media Event and Myth*. Connecticut and London: Praeger.

An informative, wide-ranging account of the Titanic disaster.

Hollings, K. (1998) 'Gojira mon amour', *Sight and Sound*, 8, 7, 20–3.

Charts the origins and development of the Japanese Godzilla movies.

Hollows, J. and M. Jancovich (eds) (1995) *Approaches to Popular Film*. Manchester: Manchester University Press.

Extremely useful chapters on the Hollywood film industry, genre and star studies.

Holliss, R. (1996) 'E – Effects', *Sight and Sound*, 6, 10, 26–30.

Succinct account of major developments in visual and special effects, beginning with earth, air, fire, and water effects in disaster movies.

Howells, R. (1999) *The Myth of the Titanic*. Basingstoke: Macmillan.
Follows the history and mythology through to resurgent interest brought about by Cameron's film.

Huggett, R. (1997) *Catastrophism: Asteroids, Comets, and Other Dynamic Events in Earth History*. London and New York: Verso.
Everything from the death of the dinosaurs to Shoemaker-Levy.

Jancovich, M. (1996) *Rational Fears: American Horror in the 1950s*. Manchester: Manchester University Press.
Explores the move from 'invasion' to 'alienation' in horror and science fiction B-movies of the 1950s.

Jeffords, S. (1993) 'Can Masculinity be Terminated?' in S. Cohan and I. R. Hark (eds) *Screening the Male: Exploring Masculinities in Hollywood Cinema*. London and New York: Routledge, 245–62.
A good introduction to the 1980s/90s action hero.

_____ (1994) *Hard Bodies: Hollywood Masculinity in the Reagan Era*. New Brunswick: Rutgers University Press.
Comprehensive development of arguments relating to the Reagan/Bush action hero.

Kaplan, F. (1975) 'Riches from Ruins', *Jump Cut*, 6, 3–4.
Lucid account of the box-office appeal of the 1970s disaster cycle, in particular The Towering Inferno and Earthquake.

Keller, A. (1999) '"Size Does Matter": Notes on *Titanic* and James Cameron as Blockbuster Auteur' In K. S. Sandler and G. Studlar (eds) *Titanic: Anatomy of a Blockbuster*. New Jersey: Rutgers University Press, 132–54.
A pithy and understanding account of Titanic as blockbuster.

Kerameos, A. and D. Sharp (1998) *Disaster Movies: Information Source Pack*. London: BFI.
An extremely valuable guide to research.

Kermode, F. (1967) *The Sense of an Ending: Studies in the Theory of Fiction*. Oxford: Oxford University Press.
Examines the narrative appeal of notions of apocalypse.

Kramer, P. (1999) 'Women First: *Titanic*, Action-Adventure Films, and Hollywood's Female Audience' in K. S. Sandler and G. Studlar (eds) *Titanic: Anatomy of a Blockbuster*. New Jersey: Rutgers University Press, 108–31.
Very good account of action-adventure films as applied through to recent action heroines and Titanic.

Lubin, D. M. (1999) *Titanic*. London: BFI.
A comprehensive account and defence of the film.

Madsen, A. (1975) *The New Hollywood: American Movies in the 1970s*. New York: Thomas Crowell.
A contemporary account of the New Hollywood with good details about the major industrial shifts of the time.

Maltby, R. (1995) *Hollywood Cinema*. Oxford: Blackwell.
Contains useful chapters on genre, industry and technology.

McClure, K. (1996) *The Fortean Times Book of the Millennium*. London: John Brown Publishing.
Aliens, apocalypse and all manner of strange phenomena.

Neale, S. (2000) *Genre and Hollywood*. London and New York: Routledge.
Excellent survey and re-evaluation of genre studies.

Negra, D. (1999) '*Titanic*, Survivalism, and the Millennial Myth', in K. S. Sandler and G. Studlar (eds) *Titanic: Anatomy of a Blockbuster*. New Jersey: Rutgers University Press, 220–38.
Interesting and useful comparisons with other millennial movies.

Newman, K. (1999) *Millennium Movies: End of the World Cinema*. London: Titan.
The cinematic story of 'destruction, desolation and devastation', particularly good on science fiction.

Pierson, M. (1999) 'CGI effects in Hollywood science-fiction cinema 1989–95: the wonder years', *Sight and Sound*, 9, 7, 158–76.
A very good account of arguments surrounding the history and development of special effects as applied through to recent science fiction films.

Pirie, D. (1996) 'Wave Theory', *Sight and Sound*, 6, 9, 26–7.
An interesting account of generic waves in relation to action, science fiction and disaster movies in 1996.

Radford, T. (1990) *The Crisis of Life on Earth: Our Legacy from the Second Millennium*. Wellingborough: Thorsons.
Presents useful environmental perspectives.

Roddick, N. (1980) 'Only the Stars Survive: Disaster Movies in the Seventies', in D. Brady (ed.) *Performance and Politics in Popular Drama: Aspects of Popular Entertainment in Theatre, Film andTelevision 1800-1976*. Cambridge: Cambridge University Press, 243–69.
The most succinct and comprehensive treatment of 1970s disaster movies.

Rogin, M. (1998) *Independence Day*. London: BFI.
An overtly political account of an overtly ideological film which turns disaster into entertainment.

Ryan, F. (1996) *Virus X: Understanding the Real Threat of the New Pandemic*. London: HarperCollins.
Focuses particularly on AIDS and the Ebola virus.

Ryan, M. and D. Kellner (1988) *Camera Politica: The Politics and Ideology of Contemporary Hollywood Film*. Bloomington and Indianapolis: Indiana University Press.
See, in particular, Chapter 2: 'Crisis Films'.

Schatz, T. (1993) 'The New Hollywood' in J. Collins (ed.) *Film Theory Goes to the Movies*. London and New York: Routledge, 19–35.
A succinct account of the various types of New Hollywood film.

Seed, D. (1999) *American Science Fiction and the Cold War*. Edinburgh: Edinburgh University Press.
Particularly good on 1950s and 1960s science fiction B-movies.

Shaffer, L. (1973) 'The Good Dumb Film', *Film Comment*, 9, 5, 52–5.
Examines the essence of The Poseidon Adventure.

Shone, T. (1998) 'Rock Bottom', *The Sunday Times* 'Culture' Supplement (9 August), 4–5.
A scathing review of Armageddon.

Smith, M. (1998) 'Theses on the Philosophy of Hollywood History', in S. Neale and M. Smith (eds) *Contemporary Hollywood Cinema*. London and New York: Routledge, 3–20.
Traces important developments from Classical Hollywood to the New Hollywood.

Sontag, S. (1965) 'The Imagination of Disaster', in *Against Interpretation, and Other Essays*, London: Andre Deutsch, 209–25.
An excellent starting point. The attraction and ultimate failure of spectacle in science fiction B-movies of the 1950s and 1960s.
Strick, P. (1998) '*Deep Impact*', *Sight and Sound*, 8, 7, 39–40.
Deep Impact as feelgood disaster movie.
Svetkey, B. (1997) 'Lava is a many-splendored thing', *Entertainment Weekly*, (25 April). On-Line. Available at: http://www.britannica.com/bcom/magazine/article/ 0,5744,13869,0.html.
A very good account of Volcano in relation to the 1990s disaster cycle.
Tasker, Y. (1993) 'Dumb Movies for Dumb People: Masculinity, the Body, and the Voice in Contemporary Cinema', in S. Cohan and I. R. Hark (eds) *Screening the Male: Exploring Masculinities in Hollywood Cinema*. London and New York: Routledge, 230-244.
A very good introduction to action movies, masculinity and the body, focusing on Die Hard.
____ (1993b) *Spectacular Bodies: Gender, Genre and the Action Cinema*. London and New York: Routledge.
Masculinity as spectacle and strong on the action genre as a whole.
Taubin, A. (1996) 'Playing It Straight', *Sight and Sound*, 6, 8, 6–7.
A succinct and comprehensive political reading of Independence Day.
Tunney, T. (1997) '*Volcano*', *Sight and Sound*, 7, 10, 62–3.
Very good comparisons and contrasts between Earthquake and Volcano.
Walker, J. (ed.) (2000) *Halliwell's Film Guide* (16th edn.). London: HarperCollins.
Cantankerous film guide with choice quotes from contemporaneous reviews.
Wollen, P. (1992) 'Delirious Projections', *Sight and Sound*, 2, 8, 24–7.
Explores cinema's fascination with the city.
Wood, R. (1986) *Hollywood from Vietnam to Reagan*. New York: Columbia University Press.
Political account of Hollywood cinema from the 1960s to the 1980s.
Wyke, M. (1997) *Projecting the Past: Ancient Rome, Cinema and History*. London and New York: Routledge.
Good chapters on Quo Vadis? and The Last Days of Pompeii.
Yacowar, M. (1977) 'The Bug in the Rug: Notes on the Disaster Genre', in B. K. Grant (ed.) *Film Genre: Theory and Criticism*. New Jersey and London: Scarecrow Press, 90–107.
An exhaustive and invaluable introduction to the history of the genre.

Useful Websites

'The Internet Movie Database' at http://www.imdb.com
Production details, cast lists, synopses and reviews of virtually every film ever made.
'Disaster Online' at http://www.members.tripod.com/~disasteronline/
The central resource for details about disaster movies old, new, classic and hybrid.
'Disaster Movies' at http://www.geocities.com/Hollywood/Bungalow/7997/
A site devoted entirely to the Airport series, The Poseidon Adventure, The Towering Inferno and Earthquake.